Monologues from Shakespeare's First Folio for Any Gender: *The Comedies*

The Applause Shakespeare Monologue Series

Other Shakespeare Titles From Applause

Once More unto the Speech Dear Friends
Volume One: The Comedies
Compiled and Edited with Commentary by Neil Freeman

Once More unto the Speech Dear Friends
Volume Two: The Histories
Compiled and Edited with Commentary by Neil Freeman

Once More unto the Speech Dear Friends
Volume Three: The Tragedies
Compiled and Edited with Commentary by Neil Freeman

The Applause First Folio in Modern Type
Prepared and Annotated by Neil Freeman

The Folio Texts
Prepared and Annotated by Neil Freeman, Each of the 36 plays of the
Applause First Folio in Modern Type individually bound

The Applause Shakespeare Library
Plays of Shakespeare Edited for Performance

Soliloquy: The Shakespeare Monologues

Monologues from Shakespeare's First Folio for Any Gender: *The Comedies*

Compilation and Commentary by
Neil Freeman

Edited by
Paul Sugarman

APPLAUSE
THEATRE & CINEMA BOOKS
Guilford, Connecticut

APPLAUSE
THEATRE & CINEMA BOOKS

An imprint of Globe Pequot, the trade division of
The Rowman & Littlefield Publishing Group, Inc.
4501 Forbes Blvd., Ste. 200
Lanham, MD 20706
www.rowman.com

Distributed by NATIONAL BOOK NETWORK

Library of Congress Cataloging-in-Publication Data available

Library of Congress Control Number: 2021944378

ISBN 978-1-4930-5676-7 (paperback)
ISBN 978-1-4930-5677-4 (ebook)

♾™ The paper used in this publication meets the minimum requirements of
American National Standard for Information Sciences—Permanence of Paper for
Printed Library Materials, ANSI/NISO Z39.48-1992

Dedication

Although Neil Freeman passed to that "undiscovered country" in 2015, his work continues to lead students and actors to a deeper understanding of Shakespeare's plays. With the exception of Shakespeare's words (and my humble foreword), the entirety of the material within these pages is Neil's. May these editions serve as a lasting legacy to a life of dedicated scholarship, and a great passion for Shakespeare.

Contents

FOREWORD

Paul Sugarman

Monologues from Shakespeare's First Folio presents the work of Neil Freeman, longtime champion of Shakespeare's First Folio, whose groundbreaking explorations into how first printings offered insights to the text in rehearsals, stage and in the classroom. This work continued with *Once More Unto the Speech Dear Friends: Monologues from Shakespeare's First Folio with Modern Text Versions for Comparison* where Neil collected over 900 monologues divided between the Comedy, History and Tragedy Published by Applause in three masterful volumes which present the original First Folio text side by side with the modern, edited version of the text. These volumes provide a massive amount of material and information. However both the literary scope, and the literal size of these volumes can be intimidating and overwhelming. This series' intent is to make the work more accessible by taking material from the encyclopediac original volumes and presenting it in an accessible workbook format.

To better focus the work for actors and students the texts are contrasted side by side with introductory notes before and commentary after to aid the exploration of the text. By comparing modern and First Folio printings, Neil points the way to gain new insights into Shakespeare's text. Editors over the centuries have "corrected" and updated the texts to make them "accessible," or "grammatically correct." In doing so they have lost vital clues and information that Shakespeare placed there for his actors. With the texts side by side, you can see where and why editors have made changes and what may have been lost in translation.

In addition to being divided into Histories, Comedies, and Tragedies, the original series further breaks down speeches by the character's designated gender, also indicating speeches appropriate for any gender. Drawing from this example, this series breaks down each original volume into four workbooks: speeches for Women of all ages, Younger Men, Older Men and Any Gender. Gender is naturally fluid for Shakespeare's characters since during his time, ALL of the characters were portrayed by males. Contemporary productions of Shakespeare commonly switch character genders (Prospero has become Prospera), in addition to presenting single gender, reverse gender and gender non-specific productions. There are certainly characters and speeches where the gender is immaterial, hence the inclusion of a volume of speeches for Any Gender. This was something that Neil had indicated in the original volumes; we are merely following his example.

Once More Unto the Speech Dear Friends was a culmination of Neil's dedicated efforts to make the First Folio more accessible and available to readers and to illuminate for actors the many clues within the Folio text, as originally published. The material in this book is drawn from that work and retains Neil's British spelling of words (i.e. capitalisation) and his extensive commentary on each speech. Neil went on to continue this work as a master teacher of Shakespeare with another series of Shakespeare editions, his 'rhythm texts' and the ebook that he published on Apple Books, *The Shakespeare Variations.*

Neil published on his own First Folio editions of the plays in modern type which were the basis the Folio Texts series published by Applause of all 36 plays in the First Folio. These individual editions all have extensive notes on the changes that modern editions had made. This material was then combined to create a complete reproduction of the First Folio in modern type, *The Applause First Folio of Shakespeare in Modern Type.* These editions make the First Folio more accessible than ever before. The examples in this book demonstrate how the clues from the First Folio will give insights to understanding and performing these speeches and why it is a worthwhile endeavour to discover the riches in the First Folio.

PREFACE AND BRIEF BACKGROUND TO THE FIRST FOLIO

WHY ANOTHER SERIES OF SOLILOQUY BOOKS?

There has been an enormous change in theatre organisation recent in the last twenty years. While the major large-scale companies have continued to flourish, many small theatre companies have come into being, leading to

- much doubling
- cross gender casting, with many one time male roles now being played legitimately by/as women in updated time-period productions
- young actors being asked to play leading roles at far earlier points in their careers

All this has meant actors should be able to demonstrate enormous flexibility rather than one limited range/style. In turn, this has meant

- a change in audition expectations
- actors are often expected to show more range than ever before
- often several shorter audition speeches are asked for instead of one or two longer ones
- sometimes the initial auditions are conducted in a shorter amount of time

Thus, to stay at the top of the game, the actor needs more knowledge of what makes the play tick, especially since

- early plays demand a different style from the later ones
- the four genres (comedy, history, tragedy, and the peculiar romances) all have different acting/textual requirements
- parts originally written for the older, more experienced actors again require a different approach from those written for the younger

ones, as the young roles, especially the female ones, were played by young actors extraordinarily skilled in the arts of rhetoric

There's now much more knowledge of how the original quarto and folio texts can add to the rehearsal exploration/acting and directing process as well as to the final performance.

Each speech is made up of four parts

- a background to the speech, placing it in the context of the play, and offering line length and an approximate timing to help you choose what might be right for any auditioning occasion
- a modern text version of the speech, with the sentence structure clearly delineated side by side with
- a folio version of the speech, where modern texts changes to the capitalization, spelling and sentence structure can be plainly seen
- a commentary explaining the differences between the two texts, and in what way the original setting can offer you more information to explore

Thus if they wish, **beginners** can explore just the background and the modern text version of the speech.

An actor experienced in exploring the Folio can make use of the background and the Folio version of the speech

And those wanting to know as many details as possible and how they could help define the deft stepping stones of the arc of the speech can use all four elements on the page.

The First Folio

(FOR LIST OF CURRENT REPRODUCTIONS SEE BIBLIOGRAPHY

The end of 1623 saw the publication of the justifiably famed First Folio (F1). The single volume, published in a run of approximately 1,000 copies at the princely sum of one pound (a tremendous risk, considering that a single play would sell at no more than six pence, one fortieth of F1's price, and that the annual salary of a schoolmaster was only ten pounds), contained thirty-six plays.

The manuscripts from which each F1 play would be printed came from a variety of sources. Some had already been printed. Some came from the playhouse complete with production details. Some had no theatrical input at all, but were handsomely copied out and easy to read. Some were supposedly very messy, complete with first draft scribbles and crossings out. Yet, as Charlton Hinman, the revered dean of First Folio studies describes F1 in the Introduction to the Norton Facsimile:

> It is of inestimable value for what it is, for what it contains. For here are preserved the masterworks of the man universally recognized as our greatest writer; and preserved, as Ben Jonson realized at the time of the original publication, not for an age but for all time.

WHAT DOES F1 REPRESENT?

- texts prepared for actors who rehearsed three days for a new play and one day for one already in the repertoire
- written in a style (rhetoric incorporating debate) so different from ours (grammatical) that many modern alterations based on grammar (or poetry) have done remarkable harm to the rhetorical/debate quality of the original text and thus to interpretations of characters at key moments of stress.
- written for an acting company the core of which steadily grew older, and whose skills and interests changed markedly over twenty years as well as for an audience whose make-up and interests likewise changed as the company grew more experienced

The whole is based upon supposedly the best documents available at the time, collected by men closest to Shakespeare throughout his career, and brought to a single printing house whose errors are now widely understood - far more than those of some of the printing houses that produced the original quartos.

TEXTUAL SOURCES FOR THE AUDITION SPEECHES

Individual modern editions consulted in the preparation of the Modern Text version of the speeches are listed in the Bibliography under the separate headings 'The Complete Works in Compendium Format' and ' The Complete Works in Separate Individual Volumes.' Most of the modern versions of the speeches are a compilation of several of these texts. However, all modern act, scene and/or line numbers refer the reader to The Riverside Shakespeare, in my opinion still the best of the complete works despite the excellent compendiums that have been published since.

The First Folio versions of the speeches are taken from a variety of already published sources, including not only all the texts listed in the 'Photostatted Reproductions in Compendium Format' section of the Bibliography, but also earlier, individually printed volumes, such as the twentieth century editions published under the collective title *The Facsimiles of Plays from The First Folio of Shakespeare* by Faber & Gwyer, and the nineteenth century editions published on behalf of The New Shakespeare Society.

INTRODUCTION

So, congratulations , you've got an audition, and for a Shakespeare play no less.

You've done all your homework, including, hopefully , reading the whole play to see the full range and development of the character.

You've got an idea of the character, the situation in which you/it finds itself (the given circumstance s); what your/its needs are (objectives/ intentions); and what you intend to do about them (action /tactics).

You've looked up all the unusual words in a good dictionary or glossary; you've turned to a well edited modern edition to find out what some of the more obscure references mean.

And those of you who understand metre and rhythm have worked on the poetic values of the speech, and you are word perfect . . .

. . . and yet it's still not working properly and/or you feel there's more to be gleaned from the text , but you're not sure what that something is or how to go about getting at it; in other words, all is not quite right, yet.

THE KEY QUESTION

What text have you been working with - a good modern text or an 'original' text, that is a copy of one of the first printings of the play?

If it's a modern text, no matter how well edited (and there are some splendid single copy editions available, see the Bibliography for further details), despite all the learned information offered, it's not surprising you feel somewhat at a loss, for there is a huge difference between the original printings (the First Folio, and the individual quartos, see

Appendix 1 for further details) and any text prepared after 1700 right up to the most modern of editions. All the post 1700 texts have been tidied-up for the modern reader to ingest silently, revamped according to the rules of correct grammar, syntax and poetry. However the 'originals' were prepared for actors speaking aloud playing characters often in a great deal of emotional and/or intellectual stress, and were set down on paper according to the very flexible rules of rhetoric and a seemingly very cavalier attitude towards the rules of grammar, and syntax, and spelling, and capitalisation, and even poetry.

Unfortunately, because of the grammatical and syntactical standardisation in place by the early 1700's, many of the quirks and oddities of the origin also have been dismissed as 'accidental' - usually as compositor error either in deciphering the original manuscript, falling prey to their own particular idosyncracies, or not having calculated correctly the amount of space needed to set the text. Modern texts dismiss the possibility that these very quirks and oddities may be by Shakespeare, hearing his characters in as much difficulty as poor Peter Quince is in *A Midsummer Night's Dream* (when he, as the Prologue, terrified and struck down by stage fright, makes a huge grammatical hash in introducing his play 'Pyramus and Thisbe' before the aristocracy, whose acceptance or otherwise, can make or break him)

> If we offend, it is with our good will.
> That you should think, we come not to offend,
> But with good will.
>   To show our simple skill,
> That is the true beginning of our end .
> Consider then, we come but in despite.
> We do not come, as minding to content you ,
> Our true intent is.
>   All for your delight
> We are not here.
>   That you should here repent you,

The Actors are at hand; and by their show,
You shall know all, that you are like to know.

(A Midsummer Night's Dream)

In many other cases in the complete works what was originally printed is equally 'peculiar,' but, unlike Peter Quince , these peculiarities are usually regularised by most modern texts.

However, this series of volumes is based on the belief - as the following will show - that most of these 'peculiarities' resulted from Shakespeare setting down for his actors the stresses, trials, and tribulations the characters are experiencing as they think and speak, and thus are theatrical gold-dust for the actor, director, scholar, teacher, and general reader alike.

THE FIRST ESSENTIAL DIFFERENCE BETWEEN THE TWO TEXTS

THINKING

A **modern** text can show

- the story line
- your character's conflict with the world at large
- your character's conflict with certain individuals within that world

but because of the very way an 'original' text was set, it can show you all this plus one key extra, the very thing that makes big speeches what they are

- the conflict within the character

WHY?

Any good playwright writes about characters in stressful situations who are often in a state of conflict not only with the world around them and the people in that world, but also within themselves. And you probably know from personal experience that when these conflicts occur peo-

Neil Freeman 21

ple do not necessarily utter the most perfect of grammatical/poetic/syntactic statements, phrases, or sentences. Joy and delight, pain and sorrow often come sweeping through in the way things are said, in the incoherence of the phrases, the running together of normally disassociated ideas, and even in the sounds of the words themselves.

The tremendous advantage of the period in which Shakespeare was setting his plays down on paper and how they first appeared in print was that when characters were rational and in control of self and situation, their phrasing and sentences (and poetic structure) would appear to be quite normal even to a modern eye - but when things were going wrong, so sentences and phrasing (and poetic structure) would become highly erratic. But the Quince type eccentricities are rarely allowed to stand. Sadly, in tidying, most modern texts usually make the text far too clean, thus setting rationality when none originally existed.

THE SECOND ESSENTIAL DIFFERENCE BETWEEN THE TWO TEXTS

SPEAKING, ARGUING, DEBATING

Having discovered what and how you/your character is thinking is only the first stage of the work - you/it then have to speak aloud, in a society that absolutely loved to speak - and not only speak ideas (content) but to speak entertainingly so as to keep listeners enthralled (and this was especially so when you have little content to offer and have to mask it somehow - think of today 's television adverts and political spin doctors as a parallel and you get the picture). Indeed one of the Elizabethan 'how to win an argument' books was very precise about this - George Puttenham, *The Art of English Poesie* (1589).

A: ELIZABETHAN SCHOOLING

All educated classes could debate/argue at the drop of a hat, for both boys (in 'petty-schools') and girls (by books and tutors) were trained in what was known overall as the art of rhetoric, which itself was split into three parts

- first, how to distinguish the real from false appearances/outward show (think of the three caskets in *The Merchant of Venice* where the language on the gold and silver caskets enticingly, and deceptively, seems to offer hopes of great personal rewards that are dashed when the language is carefully explored, whereas once the apparent threat on the lead casket is carefully analysed the reward therein is the greatest that could be hoped for)
- second, how to frame your argument on one of 'three great grounds'; honour/morality; justice/legality; and, when all else fails, expedience/practicality.
- third, how to order and phrase your argument so winsomely that your audience will vote for you no matter how good the opposition - and there were well over two hundred rules and variations by which winning could be achieved, all of which had to be assimilated before a child's education was considered over and done with.

B: THINKING ON YOUR FEET: I.E. THE QUICK, DEFT , RAPID MODIFICATION OF EACH TINY THOUGHT

The Elizabethan/therefore your character/therefore you were also trained to explore and modify your thoughts as you spoke - never would you see a sentence in its entirety and have it perfectly worked out in your mind before you spoke (unless it was a deliberately written, formal public declaration, as with the Officer of the Court in The Winter' s Tale, reading the charges against Hermione). Thus after uttering your very first phrase, you might expand it, or modify it, deny it, change it, and so on throughout the whole sentence and speech.

Neil Freeman 23

From the poet Samuel Coleridge Taylor there is a wonderful description of how Shakespeare puts thoughts together like "a serpent twisting and untwisting in its own strength," that is, with one thought springing out of the one previous. Treat each new phrase as a fresh unravelling of the serpent's coil. What is discovered (and therefore said) is only revealed as the old coil/phrase disappears revealing a new coil in its place. The new coil is the new thought. The old coil moves/disappears because the previous phrase is finished with as soon as it is spoken.

C: MODERN APPLICATION

It is very rarely we speak dispassionately in our 'real' lives, after all thoughts give rise to feelings, feelings give rise to thoughts, and we usually speak both together - unless

1/ we're trying very hard for some reason to control ourselves and not give ourselves away

2/ or the volcano of emotions within us is so strong that we cannot control ourselves, and feelings swamp thoughts

3/ and sometimes whether deliberately or unconsciously we colour words according to our feelings; the humanity behind the words so revealed is instantly understandable.

D: HOW THE ORIGINAL TEXTS NATURALLY ENHANCE/ UNDERSCORE THIS CONTROL OR RELEASE

The amazing thing about the way all Elizabethan/early Jacobean texts were first set down (the term used to describe the printed words on the page being 'orthography'), is that it was flexible, it allowed for such variations to be automatically set down without fear of grammatical repercussion.

So if Shakespeare heard Juliet's nurse working hard to try to convince Juliet that the Prince's nephew Juliet is being forced to (bigamously) marry, instead of setting the everyday normal

'O he's a lovely gentleman'

which the modern texts HAVE to set, the first printings were permitted to set

'O hee's a Lovely Gentleman'

suggesting that something might be going on inside the Nurse that causes her to release such excessive extra energy.

E: BE CAREFUL

This needs to be stressed very carefully: the orthography doesn't dictate to you/force you to accept exactly what it means. The orthography simply suggests you might want to explore this moment further or more deeply.

In other words, simply because of the flexibility with which the Elizabethans/Shakespeare could set down on paper what they heard in their minds or wanted their listeners to hear, in addition to all the modern acting necessities of character - situation, objective, intention, action, and tactics the original Shakespeare texts offer pointers to where feelings (either emotional or intellectual, or when combined together as passion, both) are also evident.

SUMMARY

BASIC APPROACH TO THE SPEECHES SHOWN BELOW

(after reading the 'background')

1/ first use the modem version shown in the first column: by doing so you can discover

- the basic plot line of what's happening to the character, and
- the first set of conflicts/obstacles impinging on the character as a result of the situation or actions of other characters
- the supposed grammatical and poetical correctnesses of the speech

2/ then you can explore

- any acting techniques you'd apply to any modem soliloquy, including establishing for the character
- the given circumstances of the scene
- their outward state of being (who they are sociologically, etc.)
- their intentions and objectives
- the resultant action and tactics they decide to pursue

3/ when this is complete, turn to the First Folio version of the text, shown on the facing page: this will help you discover and explore

- the precise thinking and debating process so essential to an understanding of any Shakespeare text
- the moments when the text is NOT grammatically or poetically as correct as the modern texts would have you believe, which will in tum help you recognise
- the moments of conflict and struggle stemming from within the character itself
- the sense of fun and enjoyment the Shakespeare language nearly always offers you no matter how dire the situation

4/ should you wish to further explore even more the differences between the two texts, the commentary that follows discusses how the First Folio has been changed, and what those alterations might mean for the human arc of the speech

NOTES ON HOW THESE SPEECHES ARE SET UP

For each of the speeches the first page will include the Background on the speech and other information including number of lines, approximate timing and who is addressed. Then will follow a spread which shows the modern text version on the left and the First Folio version on the right, followed by a page of Commentary.

PROBABLE TIMING: (shown on the Background page before the speeches begin, set below the number of lines) 0.45 = a forty-five second speech

SYMBOLS & ABBREVIATIONS IN THE COMMENTARY AND TEXT

F: the First Folio

mt.: modern texts

F # followed by a number: the number of the sentence under discussion in the First Folio version of the speech, thus F #7 would refer to the seventh sentence

mt. # followed by a numb er: the number of the sentence under discussion in the modern text version of the speech, thus mt. #5 would refer to the fifth sentence

 # /#, (e.g. 3/7): the first number refers to the number of capital letters in the passage under discussion; the second refers to the number of long spellings therein

within a quotation from the speech: / indicates where one verse line ends and a fresh one starts

[ ] : set around words in both texts when F1 sets one word , mt another

{ } : some minor alteration has been made, in a speech built up, where, a word or phrase will be changed, added, or removed

{†} : this symbol shows where a sizeable part of the text is omitted

TERMS FOUND IN THE COMMENTARY
OVERALL

1/ **orthography**: the capitalization, spellings, punctuation of the First Folio
SIGNS OF IMPORTANT DISCOVERIES/ARGUMENTS WITHIN A FIRST FOLIO SPEECH

2/ **major punctuation**: colons and semicolons: since the Shakespeare texts are based so much on the art of debate and argument, the importance of F1 's major punctuation must not be underestimated, for both the semi-colon (;) and colon (:) mark a moment of importance for the character, either for itself, as a moment of discovery or revelation, or as a key point in a discussion, argument or debate that it wishes to impress upon other characters onstage

as a rule of thumb:

a/ the more frequent colon (:) suggests that whatever the power of the point discovered or argued, the character is not side-tracked and can continue with the argument - as such, the colon can be regarded as a **logical** connection

b/ the far less frequent semicolon (;) suggests that because of the power inherent in the point discovered or argued, the character is side-tracked and momentarily loses the argument and falls back into itself or can only continue the argument with great difficulty - as such, the semicolon should be regarded as an **emotional** connection

3/ **surround phrases**: phrase(s) surrounded by major punctuation, or a combination of major punctuation and the end or beginning of a sentence: thus these phrases seem to be of especial importance for both character and speech, well worth exploring as key to the argument made and /or emotions released

DIALOGUE NOT FOUND IN THE FIRST FOLIO
∞ set where modern texts add dialogue from a quarto text which has not been included in Fl

A LOOSE RULE OF THUMB TO THE THINKING PROCESS OF A FIRST FOLIO CHARACTER

1/ mental discipline/**intellect**: a section where capitals dominate suggests that the intellectual reason ing behind what is being spoken or discovered is of more concern than the personal response beneath it

2/ feelings/**emotions**: a section where long spellings dominate suggests that the personal response to what is being spoken or discovered is of more concern than the intellectual reasoning behind it

3/ **passion**: a section where both long spellings and capitals are present in almost equal proportions suggests that both mind and emotion/feelings are inseparable, and thus the character is speaking passionately

SIGNS OF LESS THAN GRAMMATICAL THINKING WITHIN A FIRST FOLIO SPEECH

1/ **onrush**: sometimes thoughts are coming so fast that several topics are joined together as one long sentence suggesting that the F character's mind is working very quickly, or that his/her emotional state is causing some concern: most mod ern texts split such a sentence into several grammatically correct parts (the opening speech of *As You Like It* is a fine example, where F's long 18 line opening sentence is split into six): while the modern texts' resetting may be syntactically correct, the F moment is nowhere near as calm as the revisions suggest

2/ **fast-link**: sometimes F shows thoughts moving so quickly for a character that the connecting punctuation between disparate topics is merely a comma, suggesting that there is virtually no pause in springing from one idea to the next: unfortunately most modern texts rarely allow this to stand, instead replacing the obviously disturbed comma with a grammatical period, once more creating calm that it seems the original texts never intended to show

FIRST FOLIO SIGNS OF WHEN VERBAL GAME PLAYING HAS TO STOP

1/ **non-embellished:** a section with neither capitals nor long spellings suggests that what is being discovered or spoken is so important to the character that there is no time to guss it up with vocal or mental excesses: an unusual moment of self-control

2/ **short sentence:** coming out of a society where debate was second nature, man y of Shakespeare's characters speak in long sentences in which ideas are stated, explored, redefined and summarized all before moving onto the next idea in the argument, discovery or debate: the longer sentence is the sign of a rhetorically trained mind used to public speaking (oratory), but at times an idea or discovery is so startling or inevitable that length is either unnecessary or impossible to maintain : hence the occasional very important short sentence suggests that there is no time for the niceties of oratorical adornment with which to sugar the pill - verbal games are at an end and now the basic core of the issue must be faced

3/ **monosyllabic:** with English being composed of two strands, the polysyllabic (stemming from French, Italian, Latin and Greek), and the monosyllabic (from the Anglo-Saxon), each strand has two distinct functions: the polysyllabic words are often used when there is time for fanciful elaboration and rich description (which could be described as 'excessive rhetoric') while the monosyllabic occur when, literally, there is no other way of putting a basic question or comment - Juliet's "Do you love me? I know thou wilt say aye" is a classic example of both monosyllables and non-embellishment: with monosyllables, only the naked truth is being spoken, nothing is hidden

Monologues from Shakespeare's First Folio for Any Gender:
The Comedies

The Comedie of Errors
Duke {Solinus}

Merchant of Siracusa, plead no more .
1.1.3–25

Background: these are the opening lines of the play following Egeon's "Proceed Solinus to procure my fall, / And by the doome of death end woes and all", and, as with most of Shakespeare's first speeches, they are largely self explanatory. Solinus, the Duke, speaks on behalf of Ephesus, his city-state, explaining how Egeon, a prisoner, may legally be put to death simply because of his coming from Syracusa, an enemy city-state. The one thing that could save Egeon would be the payment of a large fine (emphasising the money theme so predominant throughout the play), though it appears he has not the wherewithall to be able to pay (for Solinus' change of heart, see the following speech).

Style: public address to one specific character in front of interested observers

Where: court, trial chamber, or even place of execution

To Whom: Egeon, a 'foreign' merchant: older male (father of two 23 year old sons)

# of Lines: 23

Probable Timing: 1.10 minutes

Take Note: F's orthography reveals several unexpected traits in what is often played as a flat out death sentence.

Duke {Solinus}

1   Merchant of Siracusa, plead no more .

2   I am not partial to infringe our laws ;
    The enmity and discord which of late
    Sprung from the rancorous outrage of your Duke
    To merchants, our well-dealing countrymen,
    Who, wanting guilders to redeem their lives,
    Have seal'd his rigorous statutes with their bloods,
    Excludes all pity from our threat'ning looks:
    For since the mortal and intestine jars
    Twixt thy seditious countrymen and us,
    It hath in solemn synods been decreed,
    Both by the Syracusians and our selves,
    To admit no traffic to our adverse towns:
    Nay more, if any born at Ephesus be seen
    At any Syracusian marts and fairs;
    Again, if any Syracusian born
    Come to the bay of Ephesus, he dies,
    His goods confiscate to the Dukes dispose,
    Unless a thousand marks be levied
    To quit the penalty and to ransom him .

3   Thy substance, valued at the highest rate,
    Cannot amount unto a hundred marks,
    Therefore by law thou art condemn'd to die .

Duke {Solinus}

1　Merchant of Siracusa, plead no more .

2　I am not partiall to infringe our Lawes ;
　The enmity and discord which of late
　Sprung from the rancorous outrage of your Duke,
　To Merchants our well-dealing Countrimen,
　Who wanting gilders to redeeme their lives,
　Have seal'd his rigorous statutes with their blouds,
　Excludes all pitty from our threatning lookes :
　For since the mortall and intestine jarres
　Twixt thy seditious Countrimen and us,
　It hath in solemne Synodes beene decreed,
　Both by the Siracusians and our selves,
　To admit no trafficke to our adverse townes :
　Nay more, if any borne at Ephesus
　Be seene at any Siracusian Marts and Fayres :
　Againe, if any Siracusian borne
　Come to the Bay of Ephesus, he dies :
　His goods confiscate to the Dukes dispose,
　Unlesse a thousand markes be levied
　To quit the penalty, and to ransome him :
　Thy substance, valued at the highest rate,
　Cannot amount unto a hundred Markes,
　Therefore by Law thou art condemn'd to die .

- The opening curtness of a short single line sentence

   " Merchant of Siracusa, plead no more ."

  plus the opening of F #2 with the only surround phrase in the speech

   " . I am not partiall to infringe our Lawes ;"

  suggest that for whatever reason (boredom? anger? concern?), the Duke is determined to bring matters to an end,

- yet the onrushed F #2 (somewhat diluted by modern texts' splitting it in two), and its opening emotional semicolon suggest this may not be as easy a task as might at first appear.

- While F #1 and the first four lines of F #2 are essentially factual (6/2), the next eight lines dealing with the blood feud between Ephesus and Syracusa forbidding any trade—'Who wanting gilders…our adverse townes:'—are highly emotional (3/11),

- the startling explanation of that just to be seen in each other's city means death ('Nay more if any borne at Ephesus') becomes highly passionate (7/4 in just four lines).

- However, in finishing, while remaining somewhat emotional and intellectual, Solinus seems to calm down a little (just 3/3 in the last six lines), with, as befits such a bourgeois play, the only two non-embellished lines in the speech (save for the final unit of money-measurement 'Markes') dealing with Egeon's lack of wealth which, had it been sufficient, might have ransomed him:

   "Thy substance, valued at the highest rate,/Cannot amount unto a hundred Markes,"

The Comedie of Errors
Duke

Haplesse Egeon whom the fates have markt
1.1.140–155

Background: Solinus appears to have been sufficiently moved by Egeon's story telling, (whether sincerely or no is up to each reader to judge for themselves), and though, as he explains, he cannot either pardon Egeon or waive the fine, he will allow him till sunset to range throughout the city to see if he can raise enough money for ransom.

Style: public address to one specific character in front of interested observers

Where: court, trial chamber, or even place of execution

To Whom: Egeon, a 'foreign' merchant: older male (father of two 23 year old sons)

# of Lines: 16

Probable Timing: 0.50 minutes

Take Note: Unlike the rational four sentence character most modern texts set, F's single onrushed sixteen line sentence suggests Duke Solinus is sufficiently involved in Egeon's fate for the grammatical niceties to be more than somewhat ignored.

Duke

1   Hapless Egeon, whom the fates have mark'd
     To bear the extremity of dire mishap !

2   Now trust me, were it not against our laws,
     Against my crown, my oath, my dignity,
     Which princes would they, may not disannul,
     My soul should sue as advocate for thee :
     But though thou art adjudged to the death,
     And passed sentence may not be recall'd
     But to our honor's great disparagement,
     Yet will I favor thee in what I can;
     Therefore, merchant, I'll limit thee this day
     To seek thy [health] by beneficial help.

3   Try all the friends thou hast in Ephesus;
     Beg thou, or borrow, to make up the sum,
     And live : if no, then thou art doom'd to die .

4   Jailer, take him to thy custody .

Duke

1   Haplesse Egeon whom the fates have markt
     To beare the extremitie of dire mishap :
     Now trust me, were it not against our Lawes,
     Against my Crowne, my oath, my dignity,
     Which Princes would they may not disanull,
     My soule should sue as advocate for thee :
     But though thou art adjudged to the death,
     And passed sentence may not be recal'd
     But to our honours great disparagement :
     Yet will I favour thee in what I can ;
     Therefore Marchant, Ile limit thee this day
     To seeke thy [helpe] by beneficiall helpe,
     Try all the friends thou hast in Ephesus,
     Beg thou, or borrow, to make up the summe,
     And live : if no, then thou art doom'd to die :
     Jaylor, take him to thy custodie .

- Overall, the speech is both emotional and intellectual (6/8)

- The surround phrases establish the limitations to the Duke's change of heart from speech #1 above:

   " : Yet will I favour thee in what I can ; "

   but if Egeon cannot find the ransom

   " : if no, then thou art doom'd to die : "

   the first surround phrase is extra-weighted by ending with an emotional semicolon, the second doubly-weighted by being both non-embellished and monosyllabic.

- Two more non-embellished lines detail the restraints Solinus is working under

   "But though thou art adjudged to the death,/And passed sentence may not be recal'd"

   and if the longer standard British practice of spelling of 'honours' and 'favour' is discounted the non-embellished passage would be doubled by adding the two lines

   "But to our honours great disparagement :/Yet will I favour thee in what I can;"

- Unusually, eight successive lines (three through ten) are purely iambic, with all the details Solinus wishes both Egeon and those in attendance to understand clearly emphasised by falling on the five stronger beats of each line.

The Comedie of Errors
Dromio (Local)

Return'd so soone, rather approacht too late :
between 1.2.43–67

Background: unknown to anyone, the Syracusian Antipholus has arrived in Ephesus. He is the identical-twin brother of the tardy local (Ephesean) Antipholus, whose drinking and tom-catting are currently creating such problems for his wife Adrianna. The local Dromio, sent out to bring the local Antipholus home, has in fact found the visiting Antipholus, who has just sent his companion/ servant (the visiting Dromio) off to secure their money safely in the hotel where they will be staying. The trigger to this local-Dromio speech is the visiting-Antipholus' question 'How chance thou art return'd so soone.', having mistaken the local-Dromio for his own servant. The speech deals with all the horrors back home at Adrianna's over the delay in starting a rather sumptuous lunch.

Style: part of a two-handed scene

Where: unspecified, probably a public street

To Whom: the wrong (visiting instead of local) Antipholus

# of Lines: 16

Probable Timing: 0.50 minutes

Take Note: Amazingly, no fewer than twelve of the sixteen lines are surround phrases—one of the most overwrought passages in Shakespeare.

Local Dromio

1   Return'd so soon! rather approach'd too late :
     The capon burns, the pig falls from the spit;
     The clock hath strucken twelve upon the bell :
     My mistress made it one upon my cheek :
     She is so hot, because the meat is cold :
     The meat is cold, because you come not home :
     You come not home, because you have no stomach :
     You have no stomach, having broke your fast :
     But we that know what 'tis to fast and pray,
     Are penitent for your default today .

2   I pray you jest, sir, as you sit at dinner .

3   I from my mistress come to you in post :
     If I return, I shall be post indeed :
     For she will [score] your fault upon my pate :
     [Methinks] your maw, like mine, should be your [clock],
     And strike you home without a messenger .

Local Dromio

1   Return'd so soone, rather approacht too late :
The Capon burnes, the Pig fals from the spit;
The clocke hath strucken twelve upon the bell :
My Mistris made it one upon my cheeke :
She is so hot because the meate is colde :
The meate is colde, because you come not home :
You come not home, because you have no stomacke :
You have no stomacke, having broke your fast :
But we that know what 'tis to fast and pray,
Are penitent for your default to day .

2   I pray you jest sir as you sit at dinner :
I from my Mistris come to you in post :
If I returne I shall be post indeede .

3   For she will [scoure] your fault upon my pate :
[Me thinkes] your maw, like mine, should be your [cooke],
And strike you home without a messenger .

- Given the circumstances, it's not surprising the speech is so emotional (4/15 in sixteen lines).

- The non-emebllished lines could suggest that at times when talking either about or to his supposed master (i.e. the local) Antipholus, he has to be very careful:

    "But we that know what 'tis to fast and pray,/Are penitent for your
        default to day."
    "And strike you home without a messenger."

- and it might be that Dromio loves his food, for the only semicolon within the surround phrases points first to (the horror of?) spoiled food:

    " : The Capon burnes, the Pig falls from the spit ; "

    and then to a lament that the time for lunch is well past

    " ; The clocke hath strucken twelve upon the bell : "

- F's ungrammatical sentences #2 and #3 are much more interesting than the modern syntactically correct rewrite, for with F #2 jamming together 'come home' because 'I'll be beaten otherwise' and the separate F #3 jamming together the breadth of the anticipated beating 'scoure…my pate' with 'please come home' shows far more of Dromio's concerns than the much more logical structure offered by mt. #2-3.

The Comedie of Errors
Dromio (Local)

Why Mistresse, sure my Master is horne mad.
between 2.1.57–85

Background: having been rejected and beaten by the visiting Antipholus, the local Dromio has returned to his mistress to report about the actions of his supposed (and incorrectly identified) master.

Style: as part of a three-handed scene

Where: Adrianna's home

To Whom: the two sisters Adrianna (his mistress) and Luciana

# of Lines: 20

Probable Timing: 1.00 minutes

Local Dromio

1   Why mistress, sure my master is horn-mad .

---

2   I mean not cuckold mad—
    But sure he is stark mad :
    When I desir'd him to come home to dinner,
    He ask'd me for a [thousand] marks in gold :
    "'Tis dinner-time," quoth I : "My gold !" quoth he .

3   "Your meat doth burn, "quoth I : "My gold !" quoth he .

4   "Will you come?" quoth I : " My gold !", quoth he;
    "Where is the thousand marks I gave thee, villain ? "

5   "The pig," quoth I, "is burn'd ": " My gold !", quoth he .

6   "My mistress, sir," quoth I : " Hang up thy mistress !

---

7   Quoth my master .

8   "I know," quoth he, "no house, no wife, no mistress."
    So that my arrant, due unto my tongue,
    I thank him, I bare home upon my shoulders :
    For, in conclusion, he did beat me there .

---

9   Am I so round with you, as you with me,
    That like a football you do spurn me thus ?

10 You spurn me hence, and he will spurn me hither :
    If I last in this service, you must case me in leather .

Local Dromio

1   Why Mistresse, sure my Master is horne mad..

2   I meane not Cuckold mad,
      But sure he is starke mad :
      When I desir'd him to come home to dinner,
      He ask'd me for a [hundred] markes in gold :
      'Tis dinner time, quoth I :my gold, quoth he :
      Your meat doth burne, quoth I : my gold quoth he :
      Will you come, quoth I : my gold, quoth he;
      Where is the thousand markes I gave thee villaine ?

3   The Pigge quoth I, is burn'd : my gold, quoth he :
      My mistresse, sir, quoth I : hang up thy Mistresse :
      I know not thy mistresse, out on thy mistresse .

4   Quoth my Master, I know quoth he, no house,
      no wife, no mistresse : so that my arrant due unto my
      tongue, I thanke him, I bare home upon my shoulders :
      for in conclusion, he did beat me there .

5   Am I so round with you, as you with me,
      That like a foot-ball you doe spurne me thus :
      You spurne me hence, and he will spurne me hither,
      If I last in this service, you must case me in leather .

- After the passionate opening short sentence (2/2, F #1), F's text becomes onrushed, as befits a character reporting he has just been beaten by his master, in such a way as to avoid being further beaten by his mistress: however, most modern texts do not maintain the onrush, instead splitting F #2 (the master's peculiar insistence on talking about 'the gold') into three; F #3's even weirder response to the 'Pigge' being 'burn'd' into two; F #4's reporting of the beating into two; and the final hurt dignity plea of F #5 also into two.

- Adding to the overwrought quality of the speech, the initial reporting of (the wrong) Antipholus' seemingly strange behaviours (F #2-4) is made up of an amazing thirteen surround phrases (only F #2's non-embellished lines two and three not so set) that suggest the weirdness and indignity of the situation are being hammered home (in an attempt to avoid a second beating perhaps?).

- F also sets F #4 in prose, as if the memory of the beating pushes Dromio out of the formality of verse into the immediacy of prose: most modern texts set the passage in verse as shown, removing this possibility.

- and despite all the seething emotions and needs running through the speech, a reader might be surprised that there aren't more excesses in the nineteen lines(4/15 overall): certainly F #2's last five almost unembellished lines (the monetary 'markes' and 'gold' plus 'brune' being the only exceptions)

> "When I desir'd him to come home to dinner,/He ask'd me for a
> hundred markes in gold : /'Tis dinner time, quoth I : my gold,
> quoth he : /Your meat doth burne, quoth I : my gold quoth he
> : /Will you come, quoth I: my gold, quoth he;"

and F #5's final

> "Am I so round with you, as you with me/That like a foot-ball.../If
> I last in this service, you must case me in leather."

seem to suggest that Dromio is attempting to stick to accurate verbal reporting rather than releasing a general unfocussed bleat of complaint—perhaps hoping the reporting might just help avoid the anticipated beating mentioned in speech #4 above.

The Two Gentlemen of Verona

Duke

Why Phaeton (for thou art Merops sonne)
3.1.153–169

Background: just as Protheus planned, the Duke has uncovered Valentine's plan for eloping with Silvia, including the physical elements of both a letter and a rope ladder. The opening deals with Valentine over-extending himself by reaching for a Duke's daughter—the classical reference to Phaeton is to the young man who, through over-weening ambition and envy, attempted to drive Phoebus' (the sun-God's) chariot alone, and was destroyed by Jupiter once the horses proved unmanageable and threatened both heaven and earth with fiery destruction.

Style: a speech as a two-handed scene

Where: unspecified, somewhere in the Duke's palace

To Whom: Valentine

# of Lines: 17

Probable Timing: 0.55 minutes

Take Note: Though the sentence structures match, F's orthography reveals an interesting pattern of attempted self-control with occasional emotional flashes breaking through.

Duke

1   Why, Phaeton (for thou art Merop's son)
    Wilt thou aspire to guide the heavenly car,
    And with thy daring folly burn the world ?

2   Wilt thou reach stars, because they shine on thee ?

3   Go, base intruder, over weening slave,
    Bestow thy fawning smiles on equal mates,
    And think my patience (more [than] thy desert)
    Is privilege for thy departure hence .

4   Thank me for this, more [than] for all the favors
    Which (all too much) I have bestowed on thee .

5   But if thou linger in my territories
    Longer [than] swiftest expedition
    Will give thee time to leave our royal court,
    By heaven, my wrath shall far exceed the love
    I ever bore my daughter, or thyself .

6   Be gone, I will not hear thy vain excuse,
    But as thou lov'st thy life, make speed from hence .

Duke

1   Why Phaeton (for thou art Merops sonne)
    Wilt thou aspire to guide the heavenly Car ?
    And with thy daring folly burne the world ?

2   Wilt thou reach stars, because they shine on thee ?

3   Goe base Intruder, over-weening Slave,
    Bestow thy fawning smiles on equall mates,
    And thinke my patience, (more [then] thy desert)
    Is priviledge for thy departure hence .

4   Thanke me for this, more [then] for all the favors
    Which (all too-much) I have bestowed on thee .

5   But if thou linger in my Territories
    Longer [then] swiftest expedition
    Will give thee time to leave our royall Court,
    By heaven, my wrath shall farre exceed the love
    I ever bore my daughter, or thy selfe .

6   Be gone, I will not heare thy vaine excuse,
    But as thou lov'st thy life, make speed from hence .

- At first, the Duke seems to display self control, with the opening intellectually demeaning classical comparison (F #1, 3/1), followed by the acidly precise unembellished monosyllabic short sentence enquiry 'Wilt thou reach stars, because they shine on thee?';

- then passion begins to break through, with F #3's first line dismissal (2/1 in just the one line), leading to an emotional release from thereon in (2/9 in the remaining twelve lines).

- That the Duke is still attempting to maintain control can be seen in that from now on usually only one word per line shows any release: thus, the two small clusters in the middle of F #5, 'our royall Court' and the opening of F #6 'Be gone, I will not heare thy vaine excuse' are worth exploring for extra loss of control.

- That control is difficult to maintain can be seen in that after F #2 there are only three more unembellished lines, about the favors 'Which (all too-much) I have bestowed on thee.', and the need for Valentine to leave the Court as quickly as he can , with the warning not to linger 'Longer than swiftest expedition/Will give thee time to leave…But as thou lovs't thy life, make speed from hence.'

The Taming of the Shrew

Baptista

Gentlemen, importune me no farther,
1.1.48–54, 92–104

Background: his first speech in the play, which sets up the difficulties facing the two local suitors for his youngest daughter Bianca—because, as all the locals know, the older, Kate, also known as Katherina, is such a scold that no man would willingly go near her.

Style: part of a three-handed scene, with others watching

Where: unspecified, but presumably a public place/street in Padua

To Whom: the old suitor Gremio, listed as a 'Pantelowne' (a Commed'ia type figure at his first entry), and the younger Hortentio, in front of both of his daughters Kate ('Katherina') and Bianca, with, unknown to all of them, the hidden Lucentio and Tranio watching what's going on

# of Lines: 17

Probable Timing: 0.55 minutes

Take Note: What is so startling about the speech is the totally unembellished seven line opening sentence (save for the proper name Katherina), suggesting that for some reason Baptista, is taking great efforts to remain calm (an attempt to avoid public embarrassment perhaps? or perhaps so as not to be overheard by Katherina?).

Baptista

1   Gentlemen, importune me no farther,
    For how I firmly am resolv'd you know :
    That is, not to bestow my youngest daughter
    Before I have a husband for the elder .

2   If either of you both love Katherina,
    Because I know you well, and love you well,
    Leave shall you have to court her at your pleasure .

---

3   And for I know {Bianca} taketh most delight
    In music, instruments, and poetry,
    Schoolmasters will I keep within my house,
    Fit to instruct her youth .

4   If you, Hortensio,
    Or, Signior Gremio, you, know any such,
    Prefer them hither ; for to cunning men
    I will be very kind, and liberal
    To mine own children in good bringing up,
    And so farewell .

5   Katherina, you may stay,
    For I have more to commune with Bianca .

Baptista

1   Gentlemen, importune me no farther,
     For how I firmly am resolv'd you know :
     That is, not to bestow my yongest daughter,
     Before I have a husband for the elder :
     If either of you both love Katherina,
     Because I know you well, and love you well,
     Leave shall you have to court her at your pleasure .

---

2   And for I know {Bianca} taketh most delight
     In Musicke, Instruments, and Poetry,
     Schoolemasters will I keepe within my house,
     Fit to instruct her youth .

3   If you Hortensio,
     Or signior Gremio you know any such,
     Preferre them hither : for to cunning men,
     I will be very kinde and liberall,
     To mine owne children, in good bringing up,
     And so farewell : Katherina you may stay,
     For I have more to commune with Bianca .

- This apparent need to stay calm is seen in the continuation of the speech, for the ever money-conscious Baptista seems to pulse back and forth between intellect, in the first two lines of F #2 (4/1) talking of Bianca's supposed joys in things artistic; and emotion, when talking about spending money on 'Schoolemasters' (the last two lines of F #2, 0/2).

- And this switching back and forth continues through F #3, where the direct appeal to Bianca's two rival suitors (2/0 in the first line and a half) turns again to emotion with reference to spending money ('kinde and liberall') on his own children (0/4 in the next three lines) and back to intellectual as he says farewell to all on stage, wishing to separate himself from his 'shrew' daughter, Katherina.

- Even the two intellectual passages in F #3 could be regarded as non-embellished (for all four capitalised words are proper names): if so, Baptista's struggle to maintain his sense of dignity becomes even more marked.

Loves Labours Lost

Boyet

If my observation (which very seldome lies)

between 2.1.228–249

Background: even though there has only been one short meeting between the Princesse and Ferdinand, Boyet's keen eye has already
discerned that Navar (Ferdinand) is already completely smitten.
The rhyming couplets suggest Boyet's exuberance, either at the discovery and/or simply in the delight of speaking his findings, styl-
ishly improvising the embellishment of the content as he goes.

Style: a tour-de-force aria-type speech as part of an at least five-handed
scene

Where: somewhere close to, but beyond, the palace grounds

To Whom: essentially, the Princess of France, in front of and for the
entertainment of her three Lady companions, plus perhaps any
Lords and/or servants with the French party

# of Lines: 20

Probable Timing: 1.00 minutes

Take Note: Though Boyet and this speech are often played with great
flamboyance, F's sentence structure and orthography suggest that,
though the 'aria' quality of the speech is self-evident, there may be a
deeper purpose (and character) lurking underneath.

Boyet

1   If my observation (which very seldom lies),
    By the hearts still rhetoric, disclosed with eyes,
    Deceive me not now, Navarre is infected {,}

    With that which we lovers entitle "affected " .

    ---

2   Why, all his behaviors [did] make their retire
    To the court of his eye, peeping thorough desire :
    His heart like an agot with your print impressed,
    Proud with his form, in his eye pride expressed ;
    His tongue all impatient to speak and not see,
    Did stumble with haste in his eyesight to be ;
    All senses to that sense did make their repair,
    To feel only looking on fairest of fair :
    [Methought] all his senses were lock'd in his eye,
    As jewels in crystal for some prince to buy,
    Who tend'ring their own worth from [where] they
                                        were glass'd,
    Did point [you] to buy them along as you pass'd :
    His face's own margent did cote such amazes
    That all eyes saw his eyes enchanted with gazes .

3   I'll give you Aquitaine and all that is his,
    And you give him for my sake, but one loving kiss

Boyet

1   If my observation (which very seldome lies
    By the hearts still rhetoricke, disclosed with eyes)
    Deceive me not now, Navar is infected {,}

    _____

    With that which we Lovers intitle affected .

    _____

2   Why all his behaviours [doe] make their retire,
    To the court of his eye, peeping thorough desire .

3   His hart like an Agot with your print impressed,
    Proud with his forme, in his eie pride expressed .

4   His tongue all impatient to speake and not see,
    Did stumble with haste in his eie-sight to be,
    All sences to that sence did make their repaire,
    To feele onely looking on fairest of faire :
    [Me thought] all his sences were lockt in his eye,
    As Jewels in Christall for some Prince to buy .

5   Who tendring their own worth from [whence] they
                                               were glast,
    Did point [out] to buy them along as you past .

6   His faces owne margent did coate such amazes,
    That all eyes saw his eies inchanted with gazes .

7   Ile give you Aquitaine, and all that is his,
    And you give him for my sake, but one loving Kisse .

- In F, Boyet takes a five sentence build (F #2-6) to set out all the evidence of Ferdinand ('Navar') being head over heels in love, suggesting that no matter how exuberant Boyet may be, he is still capable of shrewd and rational judgement as well as ensuring, as a good diplomat must, that other people understand what he has to say.

- In the sea of rhyming couplets, themselves a verbal sign of personal intensity, (more likely exhilaration in this case), the few unembellished lines point to Boyet's recognising Ferdinand's besottedness through what lay in his eyes

  "To the court of his eye, peeping thorough desire."

  even Ferdinand's tongue

  "Did stumble with haste in his eie-sight to be,"

  thus Ferdinand's eyes

  "Who tendring their own worth from whence they were glast,/ Did point [you] to buy them along as you past."

- as Boyet informs all the women that 'Navar is infected', he starts passionately (2/2, F #1), then becomes momentarily emotional when realising 'all his behaviours' scream of being in love (0/2, F #2), and returning to passion when beginning the more detailed analysis starting with Navar's 'hart' (1/1, F #3)

- though starting emotionally as he moves from Navar's eyes to 'All sences', (0/5 in the first four lines of F #4), Boyet finishes intellectually for the only time in the speech (3/1, the last two lines of F #4), and then comes the realisation inherent in the unembellished and thus quietly spoken F #5 that Navar's eyes plead for the Princess to 'buy' them, and thus Navar too

- from this realisation springs emotion (0/2, F #6) ending with a rather passionate, naughty-but-fun, kissing suggested finale (2/1, F #7)

A Midsommer Nights Dreame

Egeus

Full of vexation, come I, with complaint
1.1.22–45

Background: alone with his shortly to be wedded love Hippolita, the amorous Theseus is interrupted by the domestic problems of one his subjects. As such, this, the first speech for Egeus, father of the, to him, disobedient Hermia, is self-explanatory.

Style: speech of appeal for help directed to one person in front of a listening larger group who are also involved

Where: somewhere in Theseus' palace

To Whom: Duke Theseus, in front of two young male wooers (the chosen Demetrius and the unwelcome Lysander), Egeus' daughter Hermia, and Hippolita, and perhaps with court officials also in attendance, though none are indicated in the original stage directions.

# of Lines: 25

Probable Timing: 1.15 minutes

Take Note: There seems to be a tug of war between Egeus' description of the circumstances and his reaction to them, which are established either intellectually or by non-embellished phrases, and the emotional handling of the individual details of what he presumes or knows of Lysander's means of wooing his daughter.

Egeus

1　Full of vexation come I, with complaint
　　Against my child, my daughter Hermia .

2　Stand forth, Demetrius .

3　　　　　　　　　　　　　My noble lord,
　　This man hath my consent to marry her .

4　Stand forth, Lysander .

5　　　　　　　　　　　　　And, my gracious Duke,
　　This man hath bewitch'd the bosom of my child.

6　Thou, thou, Lysander, thou hast given her rhymes,
　　And interchang 'd love tokens with my child ;
　　Thou hast by moonlight at her window sung
　　With faining voice verses of faining love,
　　And stol'n the impression of her fantasy
　　With bracelets of thy hair, rings, gawds, conceits,
　　Knacks, trifles, nosegays, sweetmeats—messengers
　　Of strong prevailment in unhardened youth .

7　With cunning hast thou filch'd my daughter's heart,
　　Turn'd her obedience (which is due to me)
　　To stubborn harshness .

8　And, my gracious Duke,
　　Be it so she will not here before your Grace
　　Consent to marry with Demetrius,
　　I beg the ancient privilege of Athens :
　　As she is mine, I may dispose of her ;
　　Which shall be either to this gentleman,
　　Or to her death, according to our law
　　Immediately provided in that case .

Egeus

1　Full of vexation,. come I, with complaint
　　Against my childe, my daughter Hermia .
　　　　STAND FORTH DEMETRIUS

2　My Noble Lord,
　　This man hath my consent to marrie her .
　　　　STAND FORTH LYSANDER

3　And my gracious Duke,
　　This man hath bewitch'd the bosome of my childe :
　　Thou, thou Lysander, thou hast given her rimes,
　　And interchang'd love-tokens with my childe :
　　Thou hast by Moone-light at her window sung,
　　With faining voice, verses of faining love,
　　And stolne the impression of her fantasie,
　　With bracelets of thy haire, rings, gawdes, conceits,
　　Knackes, trifles, Nose-gaies, sweet meats (messengers
　　Of strong prevailment in unhardned youth)
　　With cunning hast thou filch'd my daughters heart,
　　Turn'd her obedience (which is due to me)
　　To stubborne harshnesse .

4　And my gracious Duke,
　　Be it so she will not heere before your Grace,
　　Consent to marrie with Demetrius,
　　I beg the ancient priviledge of Athens ;
　　As she is mine, I may dispose of her ;
　　Which shall be either to this Gentleman,
　　Or to her death, according to our Law,
　　Immediately provided in that case .

- The non-embellished lines suggest attempts at self control, not only in setting up the facts

  "Full of vexation, come I, with complaint"
  "This man hath my consent to marrie her."

  and what he wishes done if Hermia refuses to marry Demetrius

  "As she is mine, I may dispose of her;"
  "Immediately provided in that case."

  but also in both summing and then assessing the result (not the details) of Lysander's dubious wooing methods

  " . . . at her window sung/With faining voice, verses of faining love,/And stolne the impression of her fantasie,"
  "(messengers/Of strong prevailment in unhardned youth)/With cunning hast thou filch'd my daughters heart,/Turn'd her obedience (which is due to me)"

- Thus, the speech opens and closes intellectually enough (3/1, F #1-2, 6/2, F #4), but the long onrushed Lysander-accusatory sentence is quite emotional (4/8, F #3), and the three extra breath-thoughts (two in F #3, and the third before the last line of the speech) also suggest that at times Egeus needs to take an extra breath before he can voice what needs to be said.

- Yet in both there are exceptions, supporting the idea and detailing the moments of the character's inner struggle, for even in the emotionally onrushed F #3 (made much more rational by most modern texts which split the sentence into three) there are five lines of unembellished description and summation, as noted above.

A Midsommer Nights Dreame

Fairie

Whether wander I ?
2.1.2–17

Background: one of Titania's fairies (the character's first speech in the play), responding to Pucke's challenge. One note: the first line is a re-working of Pucke's enquiry.

Style: part of a two-handed scene, written partly in magic (hence the bolded text) for details, see Appendix 3

Where: somewhere in the woods

To Whom: Oberon's prime helper, Pucke

# of Lines: 13

Probable Timing: 0.45 minutes

Take Note: F1/Qq print the shaded text in four lines as shown. While the modern text version is certainly neater and creates the conventional image of a pretty and delicate creature.

Fairie

1 [Whither] wander I ?

2 Over hill, over dale,
   [Thorough] bush, [thorough] brier,
   Over park, over pale,
   [Thorough] flood, [thorough] fire,
   I do wander every where,
   Swifter then [the] moon's sphere ;
   And I serve the Fairy Queen,
   To dew her orbs upon the green .

3 The cowslips tall her pensioners be,
   In their gold coats spots you see :
   Those be rubies, fairy favors,
   In those freckles, live their savors.

4 I must go seek some dew drops here,
   And hang a pearl in every cowslips ear .

5 Farewell, thou lob of spirits; I'll be gone.

6 Our Queen and all her elves come here anon .

Fairie

1　[Whether] wander I ?

2　Over hil, over dale, [through] bush, [through] briar,
　　Over parke, over pale, [through] flood, [through] fire,
　　I do wander everie where, swifter then [ÿ] Moons sphere ;
　　And I serve the Fairy Queene, to dew her orbs upon the green .

3　The Cowslips tall, her pensioners bee,
　　In their gold coats, spots you see,
　　Those be Rubies, Fairie favors,
　　In those freckles, live their savors,
　　I must go seeke some dew drops heere,
　　And hang a pearle in every cowslips eare .

4　Farewell thou Lob of spirits, Ile be gon,
　　Our Queene and all her Elves come heere anon .

- the alterations to the line structure could mask:

  a. how the Fairie is behaving at the top of the scene (so rushed as to be unable to control or match Robin/Pucke's magic greeting)

  b. the moment of its moving momentarily into a more ritual/magical form of utterance (which follows this rushed passage)—before

  c. dropping the magical patterns in the realisation of having to go back to work

- the speech starts out with apparent calm, with a very short non-embellished F #1, followed by little or no release (the first two rhyming lines of F #2, 0/1)

- then, as the conversation refers to (brags?) of both her/his speed and describes the secrets of the 'Cowslips tall' intellect, takes over (6/2 in the last two lines of F #2 and the first four of F #3)

- with the onrush fast-link via the comma as s/he faces up to the tasks to be completed and the fact that s/he becomes fully emotional (0/4 the last two lines of F #3), it might be that s/he has suddenly remembered what s/he still has to do and is in somewhat of a tizzy, rather than offering the more rational explanation suggested by the modern texts' new sentence mt. #4

- while the farewell and notification that the Queene (Titania) is about to arrive is both factual and emotional (3/3, F #4)

A Midsommer Nights Dreame
Robin

Thou speak'st aright ;/I am that merrie wanderer of the night :
2.1.42–58

Background: the Fairie now thinks they recognise Pucke. Thus Pucke, as their kindlier alter ego Robin, responds to the Fairie's enquiring 'Either I mistake your shape and making quite…'.

Style: part of a two-handed scene

Where: somewhere in the woods

To Whom: one of Titania's fairies

# of Lines: 17

Probable Timing: 0.55 minutes

Take Note: Robin/Pucke is often played with a generalised unfocused energy. Here, F's 'ungrammatical' structure pin-points much more accurately where Robin/ Pucke is having even more fun than usual.

Robin

1   Thou speak'st aright ;
    I am that merry wanderer of the night .

2   I jest to Oberon and make him smile
    When I a fat and bean-fed horse beguile,
    Neighing in likeness of a [filly] foal;
    And sometime lurk I in a gossip's bowl,
    In very likeness of a roasted crab,
    And when she drinks, against her lips I bob,
    And on her withered dewlop pour the ale .

3   The wisest aunt, telling the saddest tale,
    Sometime for three-foot stool mistaketh me;
    Then slip I from her bum, down topples she,
    And "tailor" cries, and falls into a cough;
    And then the whole quire hold their hips and laugh,
    And waxen in their mirth, and neeze, and swear,
    A merrier hour was never wasted there .

4   But room, fairy! here comes Oberon .

Robin

1   Thou speak'st aright ;
     I am that merrie wanderer of the night :
     I jest to Oberon, and make him smile,
     When I a fat and beane-fed horse beguile,
     Neighing in likenesse of a [silly] foale,
     And sometime lurke I in a Gossips bole,
     In very likenesse of a roasted crab :
     And when she drinkes, against her lips I bob,
     And on her withered dewlop poure the Ale .

2   The wisest Aunt telling the saddest tale,
     Sometime for three-foot stoole, mistaketh me,
     Then slip I from her bum, downe topples she,
     And tailour cries, and fals into a coffe .

3   And then the whole quire hold their hips, and loffe,
     And waxen in their mirth, and neeze, and sweare,
     A merrier houre was never wasted there .

4   But roome Fairy, heere comes Oberon .

- Some modern texts join the opening to the previous line to form a single split verse line: however, the line so created would only be eight syllables long: Q1/Q2 join it to Robin/Pucke's following line thus creating an exuberant 14 or 15 syllable reply: as set in F, Pucke gives himself a splendid moment's pause before his acknowledgment—the pause offering a deceptive opening calm (1/0) for the first two lines of emphatic unembellished surround phrases and the third line.

- After that, as might be suspected with the onrush of F #1, the speech becomes splendidly (celebratory?) emotional (2/15 in thirteen lines, the remainder of F #1 through to F #3).

- The ungrammatical F #3, rejoicing in the 'whole quire's' reaction to what he set up in F #2 (the 'wisest Aunt' falling off him to the floor thinking he was a stool), allows Robin/Pucke much more of a story-telling finale than the modern texts that fold the two sentences together (mt. #3).

- Only in the final (trouble-anticipating) F #4 does intellect match emotion (2/2).

A Midsommer Nights Dreame

Pucke

Through the Forrest have I gone,
2.2.66–83

Background: having seen sad Helena abandoned by Demetrius, Oberon has told Pucke to use some of the juice of the flower to enchant Demetrius to fall (back) in love with her, telling him to find a man with 'Athenian garments'. As the following starts, Pucke is attempting to do just that, and when he does (line five) he's not to know he's stumbled across Lysander and not Demetrius.

Style: solo, and then one on one to a sleeping character, written mainly in the pattern of magic (the bolded text)

Where: somewhere in the woods

To Whom: direct audience address, and then the sleeping Lysander

# of Lines: 18

Probable Timing: 0.55 minutes

Take Note: Pucke/Robin's magic/ritual pattern (set in bold type) momentarily slips when he sees the human female (the slippage shown in normal font). This change in speaking style when faced with women is a pattern that is repeated several times later. The magic also slips later as he realises he must leave the humans (especially the woman?) to return to Oberon.

Pucke

1   Through the forest have I gone,
    But Athenian [found] I none,
    [On] whose eyes I might approve
    This flower's force in stirring love .

2   Night and silence—Who is here ?

3   Weeds of Athens he doth wear :
    This is he, my master said
    Despised the Athenian maid ;
    And here the maiden, sleeping sound,
    On the dank and dirty ground .

4   Pretty soul, she durst not lie
    Near this lack-love, this kill-courtesy .

5   Churl, upon thy eyes I throw
    All the power this charm doth owe .

6   When thou wak'st, let love forbid
    Sleep his seat on thy eyelid .

7   So awake when I am gone,
    For I must now to Oberon .

Pucke

1   Through the Forrest have I gone,
    But Athenian [finde] I none,
    [One] whose eyes I might approve
    This flowers force in stirring love .

2   Night and silence : who is heere ?

3   Weedes of Athens he doth weare :
    This is he (my master said)
    Despised the Athenian maide :
    And heere the maiden sleeping sound,
    On the danke and durty ground .

4   Pretty soule, she durst not lye
    Neere this lacke-love, this kill-curtesie .

5   Churle, upon thy eyes I throw
    All the power this charme doth owe :
    When thou wak'st, let love forbid
    Sleepe his seate on thy eye-lid .

6   So awake when I am gone :
    For I must now to Oberon .

- That his energy might be somewhat dissipated can be seen in that, while the opening two lines about going through the whole 'Forrest' are passionate (2/2), the next two, finding no-one to 'zap', are unembellished.

- Indeed, the unembellished lines spell out when and where he really has to concentrate:

    "On[e] whose eyes I might approve/This flowers force in stirring love./Night and silence:"

    "This is he (my master said)" & "upon thy eyes I throw/All the power"

    "When thou wak'st, let love forbid"

    as well as his thralldom to Oberon's will

    "For I must now to Oberon."

- the short sentence discovery of Lysander and Hermia (F #2, 0/1) leads to one more passion released three line segment (3/2) as he believes (mistakenly) that he has found the man Oberon has told him to enchant

- and then emotion floods in as first he closely examines Hermia and then zaps Lysander (0/8 in the nine lines ending F #3 through to F #5)

- the recalling of Oberon returns Pucke to a factual state (1/0)

A Midsommer Nights Dreame

Philostrate/Egeus

A play there is, my Lord, some ten words long,
between 5.1.61–81

Background: the response to Theseus' questioning: as such it is self-explanatory.

Style: a group address, directed primarily towards the Duke

Where: somewhere in the palace where a post-supper pre-wedding bed entertainment is to be offered

To Whom: Theseus, including also Hippolita, Helena and Demetrius, Hermia and Lysander, and any court retainers present

# of Lines: 20

Probable Timing: 1.00 minutes

Take Note: The Quarto and most modern texts give this speech to Philostrate, while the Folio gives it to Egeus. F suggests that Egeus has great difficulty in keeping his composure, for while he may seem to start it in relative control, his inability to keep to a regular line structure anticipates the emotional swamping that finally overtakes him.

Philostrate

1   A play there is, my lord, some ten words long,
     Which is as brief as I have known a play ;
     But by ten words, my Lord, it is too long,
     Which makes it tedious ; for in all the play
     There is not one word apt, one player fitted .

2   And tragical, my noble lord, it is ;
     For Pyramus therein doth kill himself ;
     Which when I saw rehears'd, I must confess,
     Made mine eyes water ; but more merry tears
     The passion of loud laughter never shed .

3 {†} They that do play it ,{are}
     Hard handed men that work in Athens here,
     Which never labor'd in their minds till now ;
     And now have toiled their unbreathed memories
     With this same play, against your nuptial .

4 {†} My noble lord, it is not for you .

5   I have heard
     It over, and it is nothing, nothing in the world ;
     Unless you can find sport in their intents,
     Extremely stretch'd, and conn'd with cruel pain,
     To do you service .

Egeus

1   A play there is, my Lord, some ten words long,
    Which is as breefe, as I have knowne a play ;
    But by ten words, my Lord, it is too long ;
    Which makes it tedious .

2   For in all the play,
    There is not one word apt, one Player fitted .

3   And tragicall my noble Lord it is : for Piramus
    Therein doth kill himselfe .

4   Which when I saw
    Rehearst, I must confesse, made mine eyes water :
    But more merrie teares, the passion of loud laughter
    Never shed .

5 {†} They that do play it ,{are}
    Hard handed men, that worke in Athens heere,
    Which never labour'd in their mindes till now ;
    And now have toyled their unbreathed memories
    With this same play, against your nuptiall .

6 {†} My noble Lord, it is not for you .

7   I have heard
    It over, and it is nothing, nothing in the world ;
    Unlesse you can finde sport in their intents,
    Extreamely strecht, and cond with cruell paine,
    To doe you service .

- Setting up the basic facts of the play, the speech starts out passionately (5/4, F #1-3)—at least on the surface, for the two emotional semicolons and extra breath-thoughts suggest something is about to burst forth.

- Which it does, for the rest of the speech (details and denial of suitability), is highly emotional (2/14, the twelve lines F #4-7).

- With F setting his description of the rehearsal as two sentences (F #3-4) instead of most modern texts one (mt. #2) it might be that Egeus is trying to maintain some element of self-control—which he fails to do, as the irregular line structure only too clearly shows.

- if the irregular lines (shaded, F #3-4) weren't a sufficient indicator of Egeus' disapproval/enjoyment of the Mechanicals' play 'Piramus and Thisby' the surround phrases explain why: first the emotional (semicoloned)

    " ; But by ten words, my Lord it is too long ; / Which makes it tedious . "

which, as Egeus goes on to explain

    " . And tragicall my noble Lord it is : for Piramus/Therein doth kill himselfe . / Which when I saw/Rehearst, I must confesse, made mine eyes water : / But more merrie teares, the passion of loud laughter/ Never shed . "

leading to yet another emotional response

    " . I have heard/It over, and it is nothing, nothing in the world ; "

though yet again Egeus might be attempting to establish some self-control, since the lines are unembellished

A Midsommer Nights Dreame
{Quince as} Prologue

Gentles, perchance you wonder at this show,
5.1.127–151

Background: despite Philostrate/Egeus' objections (prior speech), 'Pyramus and Thisbe' has been 'preferred' as the wedding evening's celebrations. Quince in this speech, makes a splendidly coherent introduction to both the cast of characters and the action of the play

Style: public addresses, to a large group

Where: somewhere in the palace where a post-supper pre-wedding bed entertainment is to be offered

To Whom: at least the seven royals/aristocrats plus court members, in front of at least the five members of his company

# of Lines: 25

Probable Timing: 1.15 minutes

Take Note: While the speech opens in a quiet vein, as he delves into what are for him magical details of the play so F shows his energy (and courage?) growing to a triumphant concluding finish.

{Quince as} Prologue

1   Gentles, perchance you wonder at this show;
    But wonder on till truth make all things plain.

2   This man is Pyramus, if you would know;
    This beauteous lady, Thisby is certain .

3   This man, with lime and rough-cast, doth present
    Wall, that vile Wall, which did these lovers sunder ;
    And through Wall's chink, poor souls, they are content
    To whisper .

4   At the which let no man wonder .

5   This man, with lantern, dog, and bush of thorn,
    Presenteth Moonshine ; for if you will know,
    By moonshine did these lovers think no scorn
    To meet at Ninus' tomb, there, there, to woo.

6   This [grisly] beast, which Lion hight by name
    The trusty Thisby, coming first by night,
    Did scare away, or rather did affright ;
    And as she fled, her mantle she did fall,
    Which Lion vile with bloody mouth did stain .

7   Anon comes Pyramus, sweet youth and tall,
    And finds his [trusty] Thisby's mantle slain;
    Whereat, with blade, with bloody blameful blade,
    He bravely broach'd his boiling bloody breast;
    And Thisby, tarrying in mulberry shade,
    His dagger drew, and died .

8   For all the rest,
    Let Lion, Moonshine, Wall, and lovers twain
    At large discourse, while here they do remain.

{Quince as} Prologue

1   Gentles, perchance you wonder at this show,
     But wonder on, till truth make all things plaine .

2   This man is Piramus, if you would know;
     This beauteous Lady, Thisby is certaine .

3   This man, with lyme and rough-cast, doth present
     Wall, that vile wall, which did these lovers sunder :
     And through walls chink (poor soules) they are content
     To whisper .

4   At the which, let no man wonder .

5   This man, with Lanthorne, dog, and bush of thorne,
     Presenteth moone-shine.

6   For if you will know,
     By moone-shine did these Lovers thinke no scorne
     To meet at Ninus toombe, there, there to wooe :
     This [grizy] beast (which Lyon hight by name)
     The trusty Thisby, comming first by night,
     Did scarre away, or rather did affright ,
     And as she fled, her mantle she did fall;
     Which Lyon vile with bloody mouth did staine.

7   Anon comes Piramus, sweet youth and tall,
     And findes his[ ] Thisbies Mantle slaine;
     Whereat, with blade, with bloody blamefull blade,
     He bravely broacht his boiling bloudy breast,
     And Thisby, tarrying in Mulberry shade,
     His dagger drew, and died.

8   For all the rest,
     Let Lyon, Moone-shine, Wall, and Lovers twaine,
     At large discourse, while here they doe remaine.

- As the 'leading' actors are introduced, via two emotionally created surround phrases (F #2)

    " . This man is Piramus, if you would know ; / This beauteous Lady, Thisby is certaine ."

  so the intellect starts to grow (3/1).

- The introduction of, to the company at least, the wondrous device of 'Wall' (F #-4) seems very important with:

    a. the first sentence being emotional (0/2)

    b. F #3's final line, explaining the 'chink', presented as a surround phrase

    c. F #4, advising against 'wonder', being both short and unembellished

        " : And through walls chink (poor soules) they are content / To whisper . "

- And then, with the introduction of 'moone-shine and 'Lyon' (F #5-6), Quince's emotion takes over, (5/9), with the final special effect once again presented as an (emotional) surround phrase:

    " ; Which Lyon vile with bloody mouth did staine . "

- But, with the return of Pyramus and Thisby, so his intellect matches his emotions (F #7, 5/4);

- While the almost "ta-da!" rousing summary re-introducing the support actors (F #8, 5/4) starts intellectually (5/2 in the first line and a half) and finishes emotionally (0/2 in the last line).

A Midsommer Nights Dreame
Pucke

Now the hungry Lyons rores,
5.1.371–390

Background: with the three newly married couples at last away to their beds, and the Mechanicals having left the palace, Pucke appears, setting the final scene and explaining why he is here—and for the first time speaks magic throughout without any breaks (hence the bolded text).

Style: solo, in the pattern of magic

Where: wherever in the palace the post-supper pre-wedding bed entertainment has played

To Whom: direct audience address

# of Lines: 20

Probable Timing: 1.00 minutes

Take Note: Once more the speech is spoken as the potentially more mischievous side of himself, the one known as Pucke.

{Robin as} Pucke

1   Now the hungry [lion] roars],
     And the wolf [behowls] the moon;
     Whilst the heavy ploughman snores,
     All with weary task foredone .

2   Now the wasted brands do glow,
     Whilst the screech-owl, [screeching] loud,
     Puts the wretch that lies in woe
     In remembrance of a shroud .

3   Now it is the time of night
     That the graves, all gaping wide,
     Every one lets forth his sprite,
     In the church-way paths to glide .

4   And we fairies, that do run
     By the triple Hecat's team
     From the presence of the sun,
     Following darkness like a dream,
     Now are frolic .

5   Not a mouse
     Shall disturb this hallowed house .

6   I am sent with broom before,
     To sweep the dust behind the door .

{Robin as} Pucke

1   Now the hungry [Lyons rores],
    And the Wolfe [beholds] the Moone :
    Whilest the heavy ploughman snores,
    All with weary taske fore-done .

2   Now the wasted brands doe glow,
    Whil'st the scritch-owle, [scritching] loud,
    Puts the wretch that lies in woe,
    In remembrance of a shrowd .

3   Now it is the time of night,
    That the graves, all gaping wide,
    Every one lets forth his spright,
    In the Church-way paths to glide .

4   And we Fairies, that do runne,
    By the triple Hecates teame,
    From the presence of the Sunne,
    Following darkenesse like a dreame,
    Now are frollicke ; not a Mouse
    Shall disturbe this hallowed house .

5   I am sent with broome before,
    To sweep the dust behinde the doore .

- The one surround phrase, created as it is in part by the emotional semicolon, underscores the purpose of the Fairies' visit to the palace.

    " ; not a Mouse/Shall disturbe this hallowed house . "

- The speech starts passionately (3/4, F #1), but as his mind moves towards 'the wretch' fearing the 'shrowd', so emotions begin to arise (0/3, F #2).

- The one extended moment of calm, dealing with the time of night when each grave 'lets forth his spright' (0/1, the four lines of F #3), reflects his earlier fears of the 'damned spirits all', as expressed in an entirely different way speech #29 above.

- However, realising his strength in numbers—'we Fairies'—allows time for 'frollicke', so his emotions come into play once more (4/8, F #4).

- The final couplet-enhanced statement of what his part in preparing the blessing is to be is completely emotional (0/3, F #5).

A Midsommer Nights Dreame

Robin

If we shadowes have offended,
5.1.423–438

Background: with the blessing of three newly married couples complete the Fairies have departed, leaving Pucke, as his kindlier alter ego Robin, to finish the play.

Style: solo, written in part in the pattern of magic (the bolded text)

Where: wherever in the palace the post-supper pre-wedding bed entertainment has played

To Whom: direct audience address

# of Lines: 16

Probable Timing: 0.50 minutes

Take Note: F's othography underscores the importance for the actor of Robin to seek for good future actor-audience relationships.

Robin

1   If we shadows have offended,
    Think but this, and all is mended,
    That you have but slumbered here
    While these visions did appear .

2   And this weak and idle theme,
    No more yielding but a dream,
    Gentles, do not reprehend .

3   If you pardon, we will mend .

4   And, as I am an honest Puck,
    If we have unearned luck
    Now to scape the serpent's tongue,
    We will make amends ere long :
    Else the Puck a liar call .

5   So, good night unto you all .

6   Give me your hands, if we be friends,
    And Robin shall restore amends .

Robin

1　If we shadowes have offended,
　　Thinke but this (and all is mended)
　　That you have but slumbred heere,
　　While these visions did appeare .

2　And this weake and idle theame,
　　No more yeelding but a dreame,
　　Gentles, doe not reprehend .

3　If you pardon, we will mend .

4　And as I am an honest Pucke,
　　If we have unearned lucke,
　　Now to scape the Serpents tongue,
　　We will make amends ere long :
　　Else the Pucke a lyar call .

5　So good night unto you all .

6　Give me your hands, if we be friends,
　　And Robin shall restore amends

- The two unembellished short sentences point to how calmly the actor is attempting to deal with the audience (whether out of necessity, seduction or fear is up to each actor to decide), assuring them

    "If you pardon, we will mend."

    and the wish for the audience's well-being

    "So good night unto you all."

- The other two unembellished lines reinforce the relationship further—F #4's 'We will make amends ere long;', and the opening of F #6, 'Give me your hands, if we be friends,'

- The opening attempt to apologise for any offence that might have been offered to the audience is highly emotional (0/9 in the seven lines of F #1-2).

- However, following F #3's unembellished request for pardon, the extra assurance (also unembellished) that 'We will make amends ere long' is found in the middle of a passionate five line F #4 (3/4)

- which leads to very careful final farewell-appeal (1/0, F #5-6).

The Merchant of Venice

Duke

Make roome, and let him stand before our face .
4.1.16–34

Background: this is the first and only scene for the Duke of Venice, who, having expressed his private sympathies for and directly to Anthonio, now addresses Shylocke publicly as soon as the latter enters for the hearing of his suite. As such it is self-explanatory.

Style: public address, aimed specifically at one man

Where: wherever the trial/hearing is taking place, presumably in a court or the Duke's official chambers

To Whom: Shylocke, in front of at least Anthonio, Bassanio and Gratiano, together with any other judges ('Magnificoes' as the First Folio suggests), court officials, and perhaps supporters of both Anthonio and Shylocke

# of Lines: 19

Probable Timing: 1.00 minutes

Take Note: Once more the F orthography underscores the personal concerns and humanity beneath the apparent dignity usually and automatically ascribed to the status of a character known as a 'Duke

Duke

1   Make room, and let him stand before our face .

2   Shylock, the world thinks, and I think so too,
    That thou but leadest this fashion of thy malice
    To the last hour of act, and then 'tis thought
    Thou'lt show thy mercy and remorse more strange
    Than is thy strange apparent cruelty ;
    And where thou now [exacts] the penalty,
    Which is a pound of this poor merchant's flesh,
    Thou wilt not only loose the forfeiture,
    But touch'd with [human] gentleness and love,
    Forgive a moi'ty of the principal,
    Glancing an eye of pity on his losses,
    That have of late so huddled on his back,
    Enow to press a royal merchant down,
    And pluck commiseration of his state
    From brassy bosoms and rough hearts of [flint],
    From stubborn Turks and Tartars never train'd
    To offices of tender curtesy.

3   We all expect a gentle answer, Jew !

Duke

1　Make roome, and let him stand before our face .

2　Shylocke the world thinkes, and I thinke so to
　That thou but leadest this fashion of thy mallice
　To the last houre of act, and then 'tis thought
　Thou'lt shew thy mercy and remorse more strange,
　Than is thy strange apparant cruelty ;
　And where thou now [exact'st] the penalty,
　Which is a pound of this poore Merchants flesh,
　Thou wilt not onely loose the forfeiture,
　But touch'd with [humane] gentlenesse and love :
　Forgive a moytie of the principall,
　Glancing an eye of pitty on his losses
　That have of late so hudled on his backe,
　Enow to presse a royall Merchant downe ;
　And plucke commiseration of his state
　From brassie bosomes, and rough hearts of [flints],
　From stubborne Turkes and Tarters never traind
　To offices of tender curtesie,
　We all expect a gentle answer Jew ?

- The task is not as easy for the Duke as it may first appear, and the speech is far more personally emotional (twenty-three long spellings) than intellectual (just four capitals and only three pieces of major punctuation).

- That the Duke is affected can be seen in that two of the three pieces of heavy punctuation are emotional semicolons, one following the suggestion that Shylocke's act could be seen as 'strange apparent cruelty;' and the other acknowledging that Anthonio is faced with enough horrors sufficient 'to presse a royall Merchant downe;'

- The long second sentence is a constant struggle between control and personal emotion.

  a. The first two and a half lines are emotional (0/5) as he describes Shylocke's current behavior;

  b. Then there are two and a half lines of non-embellished self-control as the Duke appeals to Shylocke's mercy;

  c. Then comes a highly emotional explosion (4/17 in 11 lines) as he expresses the hope/command (couched in the terms of generalities) that Shylocke should release Anthonio from the bond;

  d. And finally the apparent calm of F's last two lines are undermined by the comma linking them, suggesting that the final uninterrupted "We all expect a gentle answer Jew?" (as opposed to the modern comma preceding 'Jew') comes out somewhat unexpectedly and uncontrolled (exasperated perhaps at Shylocke's current non-response?): unfortunately most modern texts set the last line as a much more controlled separate sentence, mt. #3.

The Merchant of Venice

Portia

The quality of mercy is not strain'd,
4.1.184–205

Background: disguised as a lawyer, Portia has offered Shylocke the saving feminine grace of 'mercy'. He has replied that all he stands for is the masculine absolute of 'justice'. The following is her response to his rejection of her statement 'Then must the Jew be mercifull.' with the stark comment 'On what compulsion must I? Tell me that.'. Whether the famous reply is a pre-planned speech, as it so often has been performed, or a series of new thoughts and discoveries marking growing up in the world, is up to each actor and production to decide.

Style: public address, aimed specifically at one man

Where: wherever the trial/hearing is taking place, presumably in a court or the Duke's official chambers

To Whom: Shylocke, in front of at least Anthonio, Bassanio and Gratiano, Nerrissa, together with any other judges ('Magnificoes' as the First Folio suggests), court officials, and others.

# of Lines: 22

Probable Timing: 1.10 minutes

Take Note: The two occasions the F text offers onrushed sentences, which most modern texts split in two, centre on expanding the idea of mercy—first as belonging to the mighty (F #2) and—being inextricably bound up with the fundamental of (all? certainly Christian) religion, 'prayer' (F #4). This might suggest that the speech is not so oratorically cut and dried as modern texts suggest.

Portia

1　The quality of mercy is not strain'd,
　It droppeth as the gentle rain from heaven
　Upon the place beneath .

2　　　　　　　　　　　　　It is twice blest :
　It blesseth him that gives and him that takes.

3　'Tis mightiest in the mightiest, it becomes
　The throned monarch better then his crown.

4　His sceptre shows the force of temporal power,
　The attribute to awe and majesty,
　Wherein doth sit the dread and fear of kings ;
　But mercy is above this sceptred sway,
　It is enthroned in the hearts of kings,
　It is an attribute to God himself ;
　And earthly power doth then show likest God's
　When mercy seasons justice .

5　　　　　　　　　　　Therefore, Jew,
　Though justice be thy plea, consider this,
　That in the course of justice, none of us
　Should see salvation .

6　We do pray for mercy,
　And that same prayer doth teach us all to render
　The deeds of mercy.

7　　　　　　　　I have spoke thus much
　To mitigate the justice of thy plea,
　Which if thou follow, this strict [court] of Venice
　Must needs give sentence 'gainst the merchant there .

Portia

1   The quality of mercy is not strain'd,
    It droppeth as the gentle raine from heaven
    Upon the place beneath .

2   It is twice blest,
    It blesseth him that gives, and him that takes,
    'Tis mightiest in the mightiest, it becomes
    The throned Monarch better then his Crowne .

3   His Scepter shewes the force of temporall power,
    The attribute to awe and Majestie,
    Wherein doth sit the dread and feare of Kings :
    But mercy is above this sceptred sway,
    It is enthroned in the hearts of Kings,
    It is an attribute to God himselfe ;
    And earthly power doth then shew likest Gods
    When mercie seasons Justice .

4   Therefore Jew,
    Though Justice be thy plea, consider this,
    That in the course of Justice, none of us
    Should see salvation : we do pray for mercie,
    And that same prayer, doth teach us all to render
    The deeds of mercie .

5   I have spoke thus much
    To mittigate the justice of thy plea :
    Which if thou follow, this strict [course] of Venice
    Must needes give sentence 'gainst the Merchant there .

· The onrushed F #2 (split into two by most modern texts) might suggest Portia is moved by the discovery or expression of the initial idea of the first two lines, how mercy is 'twice blest': similarly, the onrush of F #4 (again split in two by most modern texts), might suggest she is working harder than her modern counterpart to get Shylock to understand how Christians are taught to 'render ... mercie'.

· Unlike most of her earlier speeches, here, in the role of lawyer, capitals outstrip longer spelled words almost two to one (14 to 8) 2 with the climax of the intellectual argument coming at the end of F #3 and the start of #4 .

· Rather than being broken up by the embellishments of personal emotion, there are several important unembellished moments, testifying to the importance of maintaining self-control, especially in the opening argument (whether this is from nerves at having to play the role of the male lawyer, the unexpected ferocity of Shylocke's response, or the seriousness of the matter at hand is up to each actress to explore)

> "The quality of mercy is not strain'd,"
> "It is twice blest, / It blesseth him that gives, and him that takes, / 'Tis mightiest in the mightiest,"

and the argument's further development

> "But mercy is above this sceptred sway, "
> "none of us / Should see salvation : we do pray for mercie, / And that same prayer, doth teach us all to render / The deeds of mercie ."

· While the single surround phrase opening the final sentence ' . I have spoke thus much / To mittigate the justice of thy plea : ' could well indicate just how hard she has worked to try, in her eyes, to save Shylocke.

· The one emotional semicolon towards the end of F #3 could well serve to show how personally important balance is to her in her own life, viz.

> " ; And earthly power doth then shew likest Gods / When mercie seasons Justice ."

The Merchant of Venice

Portia

Tarry a little, there is something else,
between 4.1.305–332

Background: with Anthonio having made his farewells and bared his breast for Shylocke's knife, at the very last minute Portia offers a completely legal saving of Anthonio's life. Again, whether her famous argument was discovered before she came to court and therefore pre-planned, as it so often has been presented, or is a wonderful series of brilliant on-stage discoveries, is up to each actress and production to decide. However, for this commentator, if it is a pre-discovered, pre-planned argument it seems very cruel to offer it so late in the proceedings.

Style: public address, aimed specifically at one man

Where: wherever the trial/hearing is taking place, presumably in a court or the Duke's official chambers

To Whom: Shylocke, in front of at least Anthonio, Bassanio and Gratiano, Nerrissa, together with any other judges ('Magnificoes' as the First Folio suggests), court officials, and perhaps supporters of both Anthonio and Shylocke

# of Lines: 17

Probable Timing: 0.55 minutes

Take Note: Having found the loophole to save Anthonio's life, despite the fascinating moments of control, the two sentence structure of F's Portia is far more spontaneous than the usual modern five sentence rewrite.

Background *101*

Portia

1   Tarry a little, there is something else .

2   This bond doth give thee here no jot of blood;
     The words expressly are "a pound of flesh ."
     [Take then] thy bond, take thou thy pound of flesh,
     But in the cutting it, if thou dost shed
     One drop of Christian blood, thy lands and goods
     Are by the laws of Venice confiscate
     Unto the state of Venice .

3   Therefore prepare thee to cut off the flesh .

4   Shed thou no blood, nor cut thou less nor more
     But just a pound of flesh .

5   If thou tak'st more
     Or less then a just pound, be it [but] so much
     As makes it light or heavy in the substance,
     Or the division of the twentieth part
     Of one poor scruple, nay, if the scale do turn
     But in the estimation of a hair,
     Thou diest, and all thy goods are confiscate .

Portia

1   Tarry a little, there is something else,
    This bond doth give thee heere no jot of bloud,
    The words expresly are a pound of flesh :
    [Then take] thy bond, take thou thy pound of flesh,
    But in the cutting it, if thou dost shed
    One drop of Christian bloud, thy lands and goods
    Are by the Lawes of Venice confiscate
    Unto the state of Venice .

---

2   Therefore prepare thee to cut off the flesh,
    Shed thou no bloud, nor cut thou lesse nor more
    But just a pound of flesh : if thou tak'st more
    Or lesse then a just pound, be it [ ]so much
    As makes it light or heavy in the substance,
    Or the devision of the twentieth part
    Of one poore scruple, nay if the scale doe turne
    But in the estimation of a hayre,
    Thou diest, and all thy goods are confiscate .

- Unlike prior speech, emotional words far outweigh capitals (11 to 4).

- All four capitals are compressed into just three lines at the end of F #1, as she reads the law which will block Shylocke.

- Unlike the five step progression of the modern text, the F speech splits neatly into just two parts—F #1's statement of the law and then F #2's incitement to Shylocke to carry out his intent but limited by the rigid restrictions of that law: the difference between the two texts seems to be, that while F's Portia is much more personally involved in the moment as herself, the modern Portia seems to be upholding and maintaining the facade of the male lawyer.

- The intrusion of the F Portia's personal responses seems to be supported by F's fast-link commas at the end of the first line of each of the two F sentences: while ungrammatical F's speedy onrush is very understandable emotionally, most modern texts replace both commas with 'correct' periods.

- Alongside the seemingly more personal responses there are moments of still calm with no embellishment, usually at the moment of her spelling out precisely what might occur if Shylocke is careless in continuing with his quest (save for the word 'devision' below)

    "The words expresly are a pound of flesh:/[Then take] thy bond, take
        thou thy pound of flesh,/But in the cutting it, if thou dost shed"
    "Therefore prepare thee to cut off the flesh"
    "be it so much/As makes it light or heavy in the substance,/Or the
        devision of the twentieth part"
    "Thou diest, and all thy goods are confiscate ."

- The two key emotional clusters underscore first her discovery or pronouncement of the legal loophole by which Shylocke will be thwarted, 'This bond doth give thee heere no jot of bloud' (0/2), and then her pointing to how carefully his weighing of Anthonio's flesh must be, for if he takes too much even by 'Of one poore scruple, nay if the scale doe turne/But in the estimation of a hayre,' (0/4), he will forfeit his life as well as his goods.

Much Ado About Nothing

Don John

I wonder that thou (being as thou saist thou art,
between 1.3.10–37

Background: Don John had led an insurrection against his eventual-ly victorious brother, Don Pedro. In the following he justifies his malevolence and current attitude to his brother to whom, however nominally, he is a prisoner.

Style: as part of a two handed scene

Where: unspecified, but presumably in quarters assigned to him at Leonato's home

To Whom: his man, Conrade

# of Lines: 17

Probable Timing: 0.55 minutes

Take Note: That F's Don John's self-definition is very dangerous can be seen in both the onrush (two F sentences compared to most modern texts' seven), and the bursts of emotional releases com-bined with many unembellished lines.

Don John

1   I wonder that thou (being as thou say'st thou art,
     born under Saturn) goest about to apply a moral me-
     dicine, to a mortifying mischief.

2   I cannot hide what I
     am : I must be sad when I have cause, and smile at no
     mans jests, eat when I have stomach, and wait for no
     mans leisure : sleep when I am drowsy, and tend on no
     mans businesse, laugh when I am merry, and claw no man
     in his humor .

   _____

3   I had rather be a canker in a hedge, [than] a rose in {my
     brother's} grace, and it better fits my blood to be disdain'd
     of all, [than] to fashion a carriage to rob love from any .

4   In
     this (though I cannot be said to be a flattering honest man)
     it must not be denied but I am a plain dealing villain.

5   I
     am trusted with a muzzle, and enfranchis'd with a clog,
     therefore I have decreed, not to sing in my cage .

6   If I had
     my mouth, I would bite : if I had my liberty, I would do
     my liking .

7   In the mean time, let me be that I am, and
     seek not to alter me .

Don John

1   I wonder that thou (being as thou saist thou art,
    borne under Saturne) goest about to apply a morall me-
    dicine, to a mortifying mischiefe : I cannot hide what I
    am : I must bee sad when I have cause, and smile at no
    mans jests, eat when I have stomacke, and wait for no
    mans leisure : sleepe when I am drowsie, and tend on no
    mans businesse, laugh when I am merry, and claw no man
    in his humor .

---

2   I had rather be a canker in a hedge, [then] a rose in {my
    Brother's} grace, and it better fits my bloud to be disdain'd
    of all, [then] to fashion a carriage to rob love from any : in
    this (though I cannot be said to be a flattering honest man)
    it must not be denied but I am a plaine dealing villaine, I
    am trusted with a mussell, and enfranchisde with a clog,
    therefore I have decreed, not to sing in my cage : if I had
    my mouth, I would bite : if I had my liberty, I would do
    my liking : in the meane time, let me be that I am, and
    seeke not to alter me .

- In the put down of Conrade F #1 starts emotionally (1/4 in the first two and a half lines) then the first unembellished phrase is followed by more emotion as John describes how he 'must be' in his various behaviours (0/4, the last four and a half lines).

- Then in describing how he wishes to be perceived in society he becomes very quiet (1/1 the first four lines of F #2), while the two lines describing himself as 'plaine dealing villaine' releases the emotions once more (0/4) before finishing quietly (0/2 the last two and a half lines).

- The surround phrases spell the character out very precisely

    : I cannot hide what I am : "

and the final

    if I had my mouth, I would bite : if I had my liberty, I would do
        my liking : in the meane time, let me be that I am, and seeke
        not to alter me . "

made all the more remarkable in that the first three are also unembellished—a very precise self-definition indeed. with the warning of"
: if I had my mouth, I would bite : ", made even more dangerous by being monosyllabic too.

- The occasional non-surround unembellished lines point to even more prickly anti-social qualities, including

    "and claw no man in his humor."

    "I had rather be a canker in a hedge,"

    "in this (though I cannot be said to be a flattering honest man)"
        "therefore I have decreed, not to sing in my cage:"

made more dangerous in their icy calm

Much Ado About Nothing
Dogberry/Kemp

Gods my life, where's the Sexton ? let him write
between 4.2.70–87

Background: having arrested Don John's men Conrade and Borachio, and put them in one of the most maladroit trial scenes Shakespeare ever wrote, the two 'malefactors' have finally lost their patience, especially Conrade, and called Dogberry (here given the prefix of 'Kemp', the name of the original actor) an 'Asse'. This is Dogberry's horrified response.

Style: public address to a large and confused group

Where: wherever the hearing for Conrade and Borachio took place

To Whom: the group at large, including the Watch, plus Conrade and Borachio, and various individuals therein

# of Lines: 15

Probable Timing: 0.50 minutes

Take Note: Given the insults just thrown his way, it's not surprising that there does seem to be a definite struggle throughout to put a cap on the hurt feelings, though the moments of forced calm in the occasional unembellished lines rarely last for long.

Kemp

1   Gods my life, where's the sexton ?

2   Let him write
     down the Prince's officer coxcomb .

3   Come, bind them .

4   Thou naughty varlet !

---

5   Dost thou not suspect my place ?

6   Dost thou not
     suspect my years?

7   O that he were here to write me
     down an ass !

8   But, masters, remember that I am an ass;
     though it be not written down, yet forget not [that] I am an
     ass .

9   No, thou villain, [thou] art full of piety as shall be prov'd
     upon thee by good witness .

10   I am a wise fellow, and
     which is more, an officer, and which is more, a houshol-
     der, and which is more, as pretty a piece of flesh as any [is]
     in Messina, and one that knows the law, go to, & a rich
     fellow enough, go to, and a fellow that hath had losses,
     and one that hath two gowns, and every thing hand-
     some about him .

11   Bring him away .

12   O that I had been writ
     down an ass !

Kemp

1   Gods my life, where's the Sexton ? let him write
downe the Princes Officer Coxcombe : come, binde them
thou naughty varlet .

---

2   Dost thou not suspect my place ? dost thou not
suspect my yeeres ?

3   O that hee were heere to write mee
downe an asse ! but masters, remember that I am an asse:
though it be not written down, yet forget not [ÿ] I am an
asse: No thou villaine, [ÿ] art full of piety as shall be prov'd
upon thee by good witnesse, I am a wise fellow, and
which is more, an officer, and which is more, a houshoulder, and which is more, as pretty a peece of flesh as any[ ] in
Messina, and one that knowes the Law, goe to, & a rich
fellow enough, goe to, and a fellow that hath had losses,
and one that hath two gownes, and every thing handsome about him : bring him away : O that I had been writ
downe an asse !

ÿ is an abbreviation in the Folio which is usually shorthand for either
you, thee, thou, thy, thine or yours

- What is surprising is the intellectual cluster that opens this speech, perhaps suggesting that he regards the barbs as doubly insulting, against himself personally and as the 'Princes Officer' who, according to the previous speech, presents 'the Princes owne person'.

- That he is deeply affected by the insult can be seen in that, though the short F #2 is unembellished till the very last word, the emotional flood-gates open (0/5 in the first line of F #3) with the rare exclamation mark concluded

  " O that hee were heere to write mee downe an asse ! "

- Then, just for a moment, either dignity or real personal hurt takes over, for there follows the unembellished double surround phrases (save for the hurtful 'asse', the final word in each phrase)

  " ! but masters remember that I am an asse: though it be not written down, yet forget not ÿ I am an asse"

  but this doesn't last, for he breaks into a passionate attack on 'thou villaine' (1/2 in just two lines).

- The struggle for self-control is seen yet again as the self-definition begins

  "I am a wise fellow, and which is more, an officer, "

  but once more this unembellished control cannot last, and the detailing of his especial qualities ('a houshoulder'; 'as pretty a peece of flesh'; and has 'two gownes') quickly moves him into strong emotion (2/6 in the next five lines), though once more he manages to control himself with the finale of self praise being stated via the unembellished 'and every thing handsome about him'.

- And though the final surround phrase order also maintains calm

  ' : bring him away : ' (a self-conscious attempt to restore some form of order perhaps), this calm is destroyed by the passionate outburst of the last surround phrase of the speech

  " : O that I had been writ down an asse ! "

  even further emphasised by the rare F exclamation mark

The Merry Wives of Windsor

Host

Peace, I say, Gallia and Gaule, French & Welch,
between 3.1.97–111

Background: having finally brought Caius and the watchers to where Evans has been waiting, the Host explains why he has deceived them both.

Style: principally to two men, as part of a group address

Where: a field in or near Frogmore, outside of Windsor

To Whom: Caius and Evans, in front of Shallow, Slender, Master Page, Simple and Rugby (servant to Mistris Quickly and thus to Caius too)

# of Lines: 13

Probable Timing: 0.45 minutes

Take Note: F sets the (shaded) opening of the speech as verse, as if the Host has to work somewhat formally to get everyone's attention, allowing him to relax into prose once he has it. Most modern texts set the more casual prose right from the start.

Host

1   Peace, I say ! Gallia and Gaul, French and
Welsh, soul-curer, and body-curer !

2   Peace, I say ! hear mine host of the Garter .

3   Am I politic?

4   Am I subtle ?

5   Am I a Machivel ?

6   Shall I lose my doctor ?

7   No, he gives me the potions
and the motions .

8   Shall I lose my parson ? my priest ?
my Sir Hugh ?

9   No, he gives me the proverbs, and the
no-verbs .

10   [Give me thy hand (terrestrial); so] .

11   Give me thy hand, celestial; so .

12   Boys of
art, I have deceiv'd you both ; I have directed you to
wrong places .

13   Your hearts are mighty, your skins are
whole, and let burnt sack be the issue .

14   Come, lay their
swords to pawn .

15   Follow me, [lads] of peace ; follow, follow, follow .

Host

1   Peace, I say, Gallia and Gaule, French & Welch,
Soule-Curer, and Body-Curer .

---

2   Peace, I say : heare mine Host of the Garter,
Am I politicke ?

3   Am I subtle ?

4   Am I a Machivell ?

5   Shall I loose my Doctor ?

6   No, hee gives me the Potions
and the Motions .

7   Shall I loose my Parson ? my Priest ?
my Sir Hugh ?

8   No, he gives me the Proverbes, and the
No-verbes .
                 [ ]

9   Give me thy hand (Celestiall) so ; Boyes of
Art, I have deceiv'd you both : I have directed you to
wrong places : your hearts are mighty, your skinnes are
whole, and let burn'd Sacke be the issue :Come, lay their
swords to pawne :Follow me, [Lad] of peace, follow, follow, follow .

- The speech starts with an interesting mix of
  - a. two unembellished appeals for calm 'Peace, I say', each time spoken without the modern texts' suggestion of a louder appeal by their addition of the exclamation mark
  - b. a tremendous intellectual name-gaming/tile-playing splurge (8/2 in the less than two lines of F #1, and first phrase of F #2).

- The speech then becomes passionate as he lists his own virtues (3/2, the remainder of F #2 through to F #4), his self-praise heightened by the short sentences, especially the last two .

- While the praise of Doctor Caius' physical gifts remains passionate (3/2, F #5-6), those of parson Evans' more moralistic ones start much more intellectually (4/1, F #7) and then finish equally passionately (2/2, F #8).

- Then it seems as if the short sentence attempts at self-control can no longer work, for as the joke on them both is revealed, so the Host finishes with a passionate onrush (F #9, 5/5) until the very last intellectual command to 'Follow' (2/0 the last line of F #9)—virtually all of F #9 being formed by at least six surround phrases: most modern texts remove this large shift by resetting F #9 as five sentences, starting the section with an extra sentence taken from the quarto, ' . Give me thy hand, (terrestrial); so . '

The Merry Wives of Windsor
Mistress Quickly

About, about :/Search Windsor Castle (Elves) within, and out .
5.5.55–75

Background: the elaborate plan to punish Falstaffe entails everyone except the Fords and Pages dressing as Fairies and pinching and burn-
ing Falstaffe with lighted tapers. To be successful they have to make
him believe that they are Fairies, and this is Mistris Quickly's first
speech as Queene of the Fairies designed to set the plot in action.

Style: public address

Where: at 'Herne the Hunter's Oake' in Windsor Forest

To Whom: the assembled company of Pistoll, Evans and various
children and young people, including Anne Page, Master Fenton,
Slender and Caius all disguised as Fairies, the watching Pages and
Fords, and all aimed to deceive Falstaffe

# of Lines: 22

Probable Timing: 1.10 minutes

Take Note: This speech has been included because it gives the actress a
chance to explore two things, the uncertainty of a woman not used
to performing to actually be the centre of attention, and then the
charm of the speech itself—the archaic quality encompassed in the
rhyming couplets that make up the speech. Thus there is no doubt
that the character is sincere, it's how successful Mistris Quickly
might be in handling the speech is what gives the greatest sense of
fun and exploration.

Mistress Quickly

1   About, about ;
    Search Windsor Castle, elves, within, and out .

2   Strew good luck, ouphes, on every sacred room,
    That it may stand till the perpetual doom
    In state as wholesome as in state 'tis fit,
    Worthy the owner, and the owner it .

3   The several chairs of order look you scour
    With juice of balm and every precious flower;
    Each fair installment, coat, and sev'ral crest,
    With loyal blazon, evermore be blest !

4   And nightly, meadow-fairies, look you sing
    Like to the Garter's compass, in a ring .

5   Th'expressure that it bears, green let it be,
    More fertile-fresh [than] all the field to see ;
    And, "Honi soit qui mal y pense" write
    In em'rald tuffs, flowr's purple, blue, and white,
    Like sapphire, pearl, and rich embroidery,
    Buckled below fair knight hood's bending knee :
    Fairies use flow'rs for their charactery.

6   Away, disperse ! but till 'tis one a'clock,
    Our dance of custom, round about the oak
    Of Herne the hunter, let us not forget .

Mistris Quickly

1 About, about :
Search Windsor Castle (Elves) within, and out .

2 Strew good lucke (Ouphes) on every sacred roome,
That it may stand till the perpetuall doome,
In state as wholsome, as in state 'tis fit,
Worthy the Owner, and the Owner it .

3 The severall Chaires of Order, looke you scowre
With juyce of Balme ; and every precious flowre,
Each faire Instalment, Coate, and sev'rall Crest,
With loyall Blazon, evermore be blest .

4 And Nightly -meadow-Fairies, looke you sing
Like to the Garters-Compasse, in a ring,
Th'expressure that it beares : Greene let it be,
More fertile-fresh [then] all the Field to see :
And, Hony Soit Qui Mal-y-Pence, write
In Emrold-tuffes, Flowres purple, blew, and white,
Like Saphire -pearle, and rich embroiderie,
Buckled below faire Knight-hoods bending knee ;
Fairies use Flowres for their characterie .

5 Away, disperse : But till 'tis one a clocke,
Our Dance of Custome, round about the Oke
Of Herne the Hunter, let us not forget .

- F's orthography seems to suggest that, for a moment or two, Mistris Quickly's being centre stage in fooling Falstaffe runs away with her; for while she opens with some semblance of control (F #1, 3/0), very soon her passions are spilling all over the stage—though eventually she does manage to bring herself under control.

- Thus, as she starts issuing instructions she becomes much more passionate, moving from the general spreading of good luck (3/4 in F #2's four lines), to much more release as details of how they should 'scowre' the 'Chaires of Order' and all the emblems of state are impressed upon them (7/10 in just the four lines of F #3), the emotional semicolon separating the two tasks emphasising the importance of both.

- The gardening instructions become more intellectual (16/7 in the nine lines of F #4), the ideas of ' : Greene let it be/More fertile-fresh then all the Field to see : ' and ' ; Fairies use Flowres for their characterie . ' being singled out as surround phrases.

- By the time of the final surround-phrase instruction, ' . Away, disperse : '—initially giving Falstaffe hope that he won't be discovered, only to be undercut by the supposedly sudden reminder that 'Our Dance of Custome' still has to be done exactly where Falstaffe is hiding 'round about the Oke/Of Herne the Hunter'—she has regained full control of self and situation (6/2, F #5).

As You Like It

LeBeau

You amaze me Ladies : I would have told
between 1.2.109–146

Background: initially their friend, the clown Touchstone, has been ordered to bring the two cousins to Duke Fredericke and the wrestling. Having been side-tracked, Le Beu has been dispatched to inform them that since they will not come to the wrestling the wrestling is about to come to them, invading their personal territory. Their obvious disinterest in the event leads to the following.

Style: as part of a four handed scene

Where: unspecified, but presumably somewhere inside or outside the palace where the two cousins meet to be alone

To Whom: Celia, Rosalind, and Touchstone

# of Lines: 17

Probable Timing: 0.55 minutes

Take Note: The fact of the early lines being unembellished or slightly intellectual suggests that Le Beu is taking great care to recover what little status he has left, especially since he has to inform Touchstone and the young women that the Duke is bringing the wrestling to the women whether they like it or not.

Le Beu

1   You amaze me, ladies .

2   I would have told
you of good wrastling, which you have lost the sight of .

---

3   I will tell you the beginning ; and if it please
your ladyships, you may see the end, for the best is yet
to do, and here where you are, they are coming to
perform it .

---

4   There comes an old man and his three sons—

{t}hree proper young men, of excellent growth
and presence .

---

5   The eldest of the three wrastled with Charles,
the Duke's wrastler, which Charles in a moment threw
him and broke three of his ribs, that there is little
hope of life in him .

6   So he serv'd the second, and so the
third .

7   Yonder they lie, the poor old man, their father,
making such pitiful dole over them that all the behol-
ders take his part with weeping .

---

8   {You } shall {† } see
this wrastling {† } if you stay here, for here is the
place appointed {† } , and they are ready to
perform it .

Le Beu

1　You amaze me Ladies : I would have told
　　you of good wrastling, which you have lost the sight of .

2　I wil tell you the beginning : and if it please
　　your Ladiships, you may see the end, for the best is yet
　　to doe, and heere where you are, they are comming to
　　performe it .

3　There comes an old man, and his three sons .

4　Three proper yong men, of excellent growth
　　and presence .

5　The eldest of the three, wrastled with Charles
　　the Dukes Wrastler, which Charles in a moment threw
　　him, and broke three of his ribbes, that there is little
　　hope of life in him : So he serv'd the second, and so the
　　third : yonder they lie, the poore old man their Father,
　　making such pittiful dole over them, that all the behol-
　　ders take his part with weeping .

6　　　　　　　　　　　　　　　{You } shall {†} see
　　this wrastling {†} if you stay heere, for heere is the
　　place appointed {†} , and they are ready to
　　performe it .

- Thus the opening three surround phrases comprising F #1 and the opening two lines of F #2 (1/0), two of which are unembellished, could suggest a put-upon character taking great care not to offend further

    "You amaze me Ladies : I would have told you of good wrastling, which you have lost the sight of. I wil tell you the beginning :"

    especially when followed by another almost unembellished line 'and if it please your Ladiships, you may see the end' (1/0).

- And following the suddenly exuberant release ending F #2, that the wrestling is coming (0/4), the ensuing short and unembellished sentences (F #3-4) suggest Le Beu is taking enormous care once more,

    "There comes an old man, and his three sons . Three proper yong men, of excellent growth and presence . The eldest of the three,"

    though whether this is out of respect for his listeners or because of the strength of his own recollection of what has just taken place is up to each actor to explore.

- As the facts are advanced of the crippling 'in a moment' defeat of the three brothers, emotions are held in check (5/1 in the four lines to the last colon of F #5), though the emphatic final surround phrase description of how Charles 'So he serv'd the second, and so the third;' suggesting that some details are still fresh in his mind.

- And then Le Beu's feelings finally break through (1/5) for both the description of the father's 'pittiful dole' and the repetition that 'heere is the place appointed' for the 'wrastling' (the last two lines of F #5 and all of F #6).

As You Like It

LeBeau

Good Sir, I do in friendship counsaile you
between 1.2.261–285

Background: as the following explains, Le Beu, one of Duke Fredericke's retinue, seems to have been as 'enchanted' by Orlando as everyone else throughout the play, though, as he explains, Le Beu fears that the Duke has not been affected in the same way. One interesting note, this is the first time Le Beu has moved from the everyday world of speaking prose into the more heightened awareness of verse, which says much about his feelings in the current situation.

Style: as part of a two-handed scene

Where: in the grounds of the Ducal palace, the favourite spot where Celia and Rosalind often meet to be alone

To Whom: Orlando

# of Lines: 24

Probable Timing: 1.15 minutes

Take Note: Given that this character is often played as an excessively flamboyant pouter-pigeon stuffed with pride, this speech shows very little excess (just 13/8 in twenty-four lines)—and if this perfectly valid characterisation is followed through, then this is equally obviously a moment where all his natural tendencies have to be reined in (for fear of being overheard perhaps?)

Le Beau

1   Good Sir, I do in friendship counsel you
     To leave this place .

2   Albeit you have deserv'd
     High commendation, true applause, and love ;
     Yet such is now the Duke's condition
     That he misconsters all that you have done .

3   The Duke is humorous—what he is indeed
     More suits you to conceive [than] I to speak of .

{Which is the Duke's daughter that was here at the
wrastling?}

---

5   Neither his daughter, if we judge by manners,
     But yet indeed the [smaller] is his daughter .

6   The other is daughter to the banish'd Duke,
     And here detain'd by her usurping uncle
     To keep his daughter company, whose loves
     Are dearer [than] the natural bond of sisters .

7   But I can tell you, that of late this Duke
     Hath ta'en displeasure 'gainst his gentle niece,
     Grounded upon no other argument
     But that the people praise her for her virtues,
     And pity her for her good father's sake ;
     And on my life his malice 'gainst the lady
     Will suddenly break forth .

8   Sir, fare you well,
     Hereafter, in a better world [than] this,
     I shall desire more love and knowledge of you .

Le Beu

1   Good Sir, I do in friendship counsaile you
    To leave this place ; Albeit you have deserv'd
    High commendation, true applause, and love ;
    Yet such is now the Dukes condition,
    That he misconsters all that you have done :
    The Duke is humorous, what he is indeede
    More suites you to conceive, [then] I to speake of .

---

2   {Which is the Duke's daughter {°}
    That was here at the Wrastling?}

---

3   Neither his daughter, if we judge by manners,
    But yet indeede the [taller] is his daughter,
    The other is daughter to the banish'd Duke,
    And here detain'd by her usurping Uncle
    To keepe his daughter companie, whose loves
    Are deerer [then] the naturall bond of Sisters :
    But I can tell you, that of late this Duke
    Hath tane displeasure 'gainst his gentle Neece,
    Grounded upon no other argument,
    But that the people praise her for her vertues,
    And pittie her, for her good Fathers sake ;
    And on my life his malice 'gainst the Lady
    Will sodainly breake forth : Sir, fare you well,
    Hereafter in a better world [then]this,
    I shall desire more love and knowledge of you .

- The onrush of both sentences F #1 and especially F #3, are testimony to the pressure Le Beu is feeling, though the modern texts create a much more rational character throughout, splitting F #1 into three sentences and F #3 into four.

- The four extra breath-thoughts all seem to come as extra key information is being offered, such as adding the final doom-laden details, viz.

   ", / That he misconsters all that you have done : "

   ", then I to speake of . "

   ", But that the people praise her for her vertues, / And pittie her, for her good Fathers sake ; "

- The semicolon created emotional surround phrases point to the fears for both Orlando's safety

   " . Good Sir, I do in friendship counsaile you / To leave this place ; Albeit you have deserv'd / High commendation, true applause, and love ; "

and for Rosalind, both stemming from the Duke's inner nature

   " ; And on my life his malice 'gainst the Lady / Will sodainly breake forth : "

- As the single emotional cluster refers to the affection between the cousins Rosalind and Celia 'whose loves / Are deerer then the naturall bond of Sisters', it's quite fascinating to see that ten of Le Beu's thirteen capitals refer in one way or another to the relationships between the two young women and their respective fathers.

As You Like It

Duke Frederick

I Celia, we staid her for your sake,
between 1.3.67–89

Background: in addition to having banished her father, his brother, Fredricke has now banished his niece Rosalind too, and has been challenged publicly by his daughter Celia. His reasons, as explained below, might have been triggered by an incident at the wrestling, where, after Le Beu had indicated to Orlando that 'the Princesse cals for you', one of two unfortunate things took place: either Orlando did not address himself to Celia as he should have but addressed Rosalind instead, or Rosalind herself in her impetuosity asked the first question, as she would have done had she still been the rightful princess—either way it's possible Fredricke feels his daughter was publicly slighted.

Style: as part of a three-handed scene in front of others

Where: unspecified, but presumably somewhere inside or outside the palace where the two cousins meet to be alone

To Whom: Celia and then Rosalind in front of members of Fredricke's retinue

# of Lines: 13

Probable Timing: 0.45 minutes

Take Note: Despite the proportionately large number of unembellished lines and accompanying relative lack of release, the onrushed mid-sentence F #2 and extra breath-thoughts suggest that Celia's father's apparent calm is only maintained with great difficulty.

Duke Fredricke

1   Ay, Celia, we stay'd her for your sake,
        Else had she with her father rang'd along .

---

2   She is too subtile for thee, and her smoothness,
        Her very silence and her patience
        Speak to the people, and they pity her .

3   Thou art a fool; she robs thee of thy name,
        And thou wilt show more bright & seem more virtuous
        When she is gone .

4   Then open not thy lips :
        Firm and irrevocable is my doom
        Which I have pass'd upon her ; she is banish'd .

---

5 {†}   You, niece, provide yourself;
        If you outstay the time, upon mine honor,
        And in the greatness of my word, you die .

Duke Fredricke

1   I Celia, we staid her for your sake,
     Else had she with her Father rang'd along .

———————————————————

2   She is too subtile for thee, and her smoothnes ;
     Her verie silence, and her patience,
     Speake to the people, and they pittie her :
     Thou art a foole, she robs thee of thy name,
     And thou wilt show more bright, & seem more vertuous
     When she is gone : then open not thy lips
     Firme, and irrevocable is my doombe
     Which I have past upon her, she is banish'd .

———————————————————

3 {†} You Neice provide your selfe,
     If you out-stay the time, upon mine honor,
     And in the greatnesse of my word you die .

- The one (unembellished) surround-phrase says it all:

  " . She is too subtile for thee, and her smoothnes ; "

  especially when it is cut off in mid thought by the grammatically appalling F only emotional semicolon.

- Given their powerful content, the remaining unembellished lines could well suggest that no matter how misguided, her father is very sincere in his actions and really wants her to understand why he is banishing Rosalind,

  "Her verie silence, and her patience . . . / . . . robs thee of thy name,/ And thou wilt show more bright, . . . /When she is gone: then open not thy lips"

  his final words to Rosalind leaving no doubt how far he is prepared to go:

  "If you out-stay the time, upon mine honor, . . . you die."

- The speech opens factually (2/0, F #1), while the onrushed F #2 shows just three emotional lines breaking the enforced calm (0/5 in eight lines), with emotion slightly outweighing facts in the final act of banishment (1/2, F #3).

As You Like It

Jacques

A Foole, a foole : I met a foole i'th Forrest,
2.7.12–34

Background: Jaques seems to be always looking for someone new to talk to, and is always eager, at least at the beginning of a scene (perhaps the high end of a bi-polar condition, a modern equivalency for the Elizabethan term 'melancholy'), for some form of intelligent disputive conversation. Here, having just met offstage the clown Touchstone, Jaques seems even more animated than usual (hence Duke Senior's seemingly amazed comment ('What, you look merrily')).

Style: address to a group

Where: at Duke Senior's encampment

To Whom: Duke Senior, Amiens, and Duke Senior's followers

# of Lines: 23

Probable Timing: 1.10 minutes

Take Note: The importance of his meeting Touchstone can be seen in the onrushed opening of the speech (split into five sentences by modern texts) starting with two highly passionate surround phrases, just in setting up the very briefest of the circumstances; the new onrush of F #2's details of the meeting and conversation (reduced in impact by being split into five separate sentences by most modern texts); and the last two highly emotional surround phrases ending the speech (1/5), extolling the virtues of the 'worthy foole' and that essentially to be a 'foole' is the very best thing for the age ('Motley's the only weare').

Jaques

1   A Fool, a fool!

2   I met a fool i'th forest,

3   A motley fool .

4   (A miserable world !)

5   As I do live by food, I met a fool,
    Who laid him down, and bask'd him in the sun,
    And rail'd on Lady Fortune in good terms,
    In good set terms, and yet a motley fool .

6   "Good morrow, fool, " quoth I .

7   "No, Sir", quoth he,
    "Call me not fool till heaven hath sent me fortune ."

8   And then he drew a dial from his poke,
    And looking on it, with lack-lustre eye,
    Says, very wisely, "it is ten a clock ."

9   "Thus we may see," quoth he, "how the world wags."

10 'Tis but an hour ago since it was nine,
    And after one hour more 'twill be eleven,
    And so from hour to hour, we ripe and ripe,
    And then from hour to hour, we rot and rot ;
    And thereby hangs a tale" .

11   When I did hear
    The motley fool thus moral on the time,
    My lungs began to crow like chanticleer,
    That fools should be so deep contemplative ;
    And I did laugh, sans intermission
    An hour by his dial .

12   O noble fool!

13 A worthy fool!

14   Motley's the only wear .

Jaques

1   A Foole, a foole : I met a foole i'th Forrest,
A motley Foole (a miserable world :)
As I do live by foode, I met a foole,
Who laid him downe, and bask'd him in the Sun,
And rail'd on Lady Fortune in good termes,
In good set termes, and yet a motley foole .

2   Good morrow foole (quoth I :) no Sir, quoth he,
Call me not foole, till heaven hath sent me fortune,
And then he drew a diall from his poake,
And looking on it, with lacke-lustre eye,
Sayes, very wisely, it is ten a clocke :
Thus we may see (quoth he) how the world wagges :
'Tis but an houre agoe, since it was nine,
And after one houre more, 'twill be eleven,
And so from houre to houre, we ripe, and ripe,
And then from houre to houre, we rot, and rot,
And thereby hangs a tale .

3   When I did heare
The motley Foole, thus morall on the time,
My Lungs began to crow like Chanticleere,
That Fooles should be so deepe contemplative :
And I did laugh, sans intermission
An houre by his diall .

4   Oh noble foole,
A worthy foole : Motley's the onely weare .

- The passion of the first two lines (3/5) is continued as Jaques describes in general how the 'foole' presented himself (3/6 the last four lines of F #1).

- Then, as the details are piled one on top of another in the long F #2, so emotion takes over completely—with the exception of the one capitalised word 'Sir' (1/13 in ten and a half lines).

- The description of Touchstone's sententious comments about life and time (the last five and a half lines) are suddenly punctuated by four extra breath-thoughts, though whether Jaques needs these for control to prevent himself from laughing, or simply to make sure he can get his amazed response over to his listeners is up to each actor to explore.

- Then, as Jaques describes his own response to what Touchstone said, so passion returns (4/4 in the first three and a half lines of F #3).

- Interestingly, the incredibly simple and short monosyllabic phrase testifying to his laughter ("And I did laugh') is one of the very few unembellished lines or phrases in the speech;

- but, with the final praise of the 'foole', this quickly gives way to enormous emotion once more (1/7 in the last two lines of the speech).

As You Like It

Jacques

I am ambitious for a motley coat ./It is my onely suite,
between 2.7 43–61

Background: the meeting with Touchstone seems to have triggered in Jaques an understanding of how he would like to conduct the remainder of his life. One note: the 'motley coat' was a multi-coloured, often patched, coat that licensed fools and jesters would wear as a symbol of their profession.

Style: one on one in front of a larger group

Where: at Duke Senior's encampment

To Whom: Duke Senior, in front of Amiens and an undetermined number of Duke Senior's followers

# of Lines: 19

Probable Timing: 1.00 minutes

Take Note: With Jaques' demonstrated ability to suddenly discover things about himself in the middle of conversations, it may be that, since the opening sentence is both short and unembellished, the realisation that he is 'ambitious for a motley coat' has either just struck him, or he is voicing it carefully and quietly to the Duke as a very serious proposition.

Jaques

1   I am ambitious for a motley coat .

---

2   It is my only suit-
Provided that you weed your better judgments
Of all opinion that grows rank in them,
That I am wise .

3   I must have liberty
Withal, as large a charter as the wind,
To blow on whom I please, for so fools have ;
And they that are most galled with my folly,
They most must laugh .

4   And why, sir, must they so ?

5   The why is plain as way to parish church :
He that a fool doth very wisely hit
Doth very foolishly, although he smart,
[Not to] seem senseless of the bob ; if not,
The wise man's folly is anatomiz'd
Even by the squand'ring glances of the fool.

6   Invest me in my motley ; give me leave
To speak my mind, and I will through and through
Cleanse the foul body of th'infected world,
If they will patiently receive my medicine .

Jaques

1   I am ambitious for a motley coat .

---

2   It is my onely suite,
    Provided that you weed your better judgements
    Of all opinion that growes ranke in them,
    That I am wise .

3   I must have liberty
    Withall, as large a Charter as the winde,
    To blow on whom I please, for so fooles have :
    And they that are most gauled with my folly,
    They most must laugh : And why sir must they so ?

4   The why is plaine, as way to Parish Church :
    Hee, that a Foole doth very wisely hit,
    Doth very foolishly, although he smart
    [ ] Seeme senselesse of the bob .

5   If not,
    The Wise-mans folly is anathomiz'd
    Even by the squandring glances of the foole .

6   Invest me in my motley : Give me leave
    To speake my minde, and I will through and through
    Cleanse the foule bodie of th'infected world,
    If they will patiently receive my medicine .

- As Jaques begins to explain the scope of what he wants, so he becomes emotional (1/8, F #2 and the first two and a half lines of F #3).

- It looks as if Jaques has got either some specific targets in mind, or has great fancies as to what he might be able to do as a 'foole', for the introduction of 'And they that are most gauled with my folly,/ They most must laugh' is unembellished and a surround phrase, and the embellishment of the idea continues the hard-working surround-phrase means of expression and becomes intellectual (3/1).

  " : And why sir must they so ? / The why is plaine, as way to Parish Church : "

- Then, as Jaques becomes more specific with 'Hee that a Foole…' he turns emotional once more (1/4, the last three lines of F #4).

- The idea of embarrassing even the 'Wise-man' simply by a look once more drives Jaques into an almost completely unembellished anticipation (1/1, F #5), leading to yet another unembellished surround phrase (demanding? pleading?) 'Invest me in my motley . ' , leading again to emotion as to how to cleanse the 'foule bodie of th'infected world' (1/3, the next two and a half lines of the final sentence).

- However, the last line reverie/hope of what he might achieve 'If they will patiently receive my medicine' is once more spoken without embellishment (a dream or plea once more?).

Not see him since ? Sir, sir, that cannot be :
between 3.1.1–18

Background: Duke Fredricke's retinue have found that Orlando has disappeared too, and thus have brought Oliver (Orlando's older brother) in for questioning. This speech, which starts the scene, suggests that Fredricke's questioning began somewhere offstage before the onstage scene started.

Style: one on one, in front of a small group

Where: somewhere in the palace

To Whom: Oliver, in front of members of his retinue

# of Lines: 15

Probable Timing: 0.50 minutes

Take Note: That Duke Fredricke seems to deliberately employ a browbeating tactic of a sudden outburst in the sea of his usual calm is once more seen here, as is his tendency to employ as few sentences as possible to get his points across.

Duke Fredricke

1   Not see him since ?

2   Sir, sir, that cannot be .

3   But were I not the better part made mercy,
    I should not seek an absent argument
    Of my revenge, thou present .

4   But look to it :
    Find out thy brother, wheresoe'er he is ;
    Seek him with candle ; bring him dead or living
    Within this twelvemonth, or turn thou no more
    To seek a living in our territory .

5   Thy lands and all things that thou dost call thine
    Worth seizure do we seize into our hands,
    Till thou canst quit thee by thy brother's mouth,
    Of what we think against thee .

---

6   Well, push him out of doors,
    And let my officers of such a nature
    Make an extent upon his house and lands .
    Do this expediently, and turn him going .

Duke Fredricke

1　Not see him since ?

2　　　　　　　　　　Sir, sir, that cannot be :
But were I not the better part made mercie,
I should not seeke an absent argument
Of my revenge, thou present : but looke to it,
Finde out thy brother wheresoere he is,
Seeke him with Candle : bring him dead, or living
Within this twelvemonth, or turne thou no more
To seek a living in our Territorie .

3　Thy Lands and all things that thou dost call thine,
Worth seizure, do we seize into our hands,
Till thou canst quit thee by thy brothers mouth,
Of what we thinke against thee .

4　　　　　　　　　　Well push him out of dores
And let my officers of such a nature
Make an extent upon his house and Lands :
Do this expediently, and turne him going .

- The first three and a half lines, not only denying what Oliver might have said but threatening him too, are totally unembellished: yet the firmness of the denial is beyond question, beginning with a short (unembellished) monosyllabic sentence/question (F #1), which is then reinforced straightaway by an (unembellished) surround phrase (the opening of F #2).

- The calm is suddenly destroyed, but only momentarily, by the command to 'Finde out' Orlando (1/4 in just two lines), to be immediately followed by yet another unembellished line ferocious in its calmness:

    ": bring him dead, or living/Within this twelvemonth,"

    enhanced by the extra breath-thought.

- Then comes yet another small, this time factual, explosion (2/1) highlighting Oliver's potential banishment (the end of F #2) and the very definite and immediate seizure of all his property as a forfeit until successful (the first line of F #4); again the extra breath-thoughts, rather than more excessive vocal releases, reinforce all the necessary details,

- and the final six and a half lines of the speech, tidying-up the details and getting rid of Oliver, become relatively calm once more (just three of the lines showing any excess, 1/2).

As You Like It

Corin

{†} I know the more one sickens, the worse at ease he is :
3.2.23–31 plus 3.2.73–77

Background: Corin's response to Touchstone's blatant question, 'Has't any Philosophie in thee shepheard?'. One note: sentence F #3 originally followed Touchstone's teasing suggestion that Corin may be 'damn'd'– in the context of this speech the sentence could be triggered by supposed laughter from Corin's scene partner.

Style: as part of a two-handed scene

Where: somewhere in the woods, near the cottage of Rosalind and Celia

To Whom: Touchstone

# of Lines: 13

Probable Timing: 0.45 minutes

Take Note: The capital letters in the Folio highlight the main points of Corin's philosophy.

Corin

1 {†}   I know the more one sickens
the worse at ease he is ; and that he that wants money,
means, and content is without three good friends; that
the property of rain is to wet and fire to burn ; That
good pasture makes fat sheep; and that a great cause of
the night is lack of the Sun; that he that hath learned no wit by nature, nor art, may complain of good
breeding, or comes of a very dull kindred .

---

2 {†} I am a true laborer: I earn that I eat, get
that I wear, owe no man hate, envy no mans happi-
ness, glad of other men's good, content with my harm,
and the greatest of my pride, is to see my ewes graze &
my lambs suck .

Corin

1 {†}   I know the more one sickens,
    the worse at ease he is : and that hee that wants money,
    meanes, and content, is without three good frends .

2   That
    the propertie of raine is to wet, and fire to burne : That
    good pasture makes fat sheepe : and that a great cause of
    the night, is lacke of the Sunne : That hee that hath lear-
    ned no wit by Nature, nor Art, may complaine of good
    breeding, or comes of a very dull kindred .

---

3 {†}   I am a true Labourer, I earne that I eate : get
    that I weare ; owe no man hate, envie no mans happi-
    nesse ; glad of other mens good content with my harme :
    and the greatest of my pride, is to see my Ewes graze, &
                      my Lambes sucke .

- That perhaps Corin only eventually finds a way to triumph in his 'Philosophie' might be seen in the build—first F #1's quiet start with four of six phrases being unembellished; then the growth first to emotion (0/5, F #1 and the first two lines of F #2); and then the moment of slight passion(1/1 in one line) over 'night' being caused by 'the lacke of the Sunne', which leads to his final much more passionate two line flourish with its sly dig at 'good breeding' (3/2 F #2).

- That this starts as hard work for him might be seen in the five surround phrases/lines that open the speech, and the two extra breath-thoughts by which he strains to add the necessary extra detail to the point being made.

- However, his strong self-definition of F #3 is a very different matter, with emotion flowing from the very start (1/6 in the first three lines), the emotion further heightened with three of the five surround phrases formed in part by the emotional semicolons.

- Thus it's interesting to see the (dignified?) ending as he describes his greatest pride (2/1, the last line and a half).

Twelfe Night, or what you will

Fabian

This was a great argument of love in her toward you .

between 3.2.11–29

Background: Andrew is on the point of abandoning his wooing of Olivia yet again, this time because of Olivia's obvious interest in Cesario/Viola. As Andrew tells Toby, 'Marry I saw your Neece do more favours to the Counts Serving-man, then ever she bestow'd upon mee: I saw't i'th'Orchard.'. Toby's henchman Fabian hastily attempts to repair the damage.

Style: as part of a three-handed scene

Where: somewhere in Olivia's home or gardens

To Whom: Sir Andrew, in front of Sir Toby

# of Lines: 12

Probable Timing: 0.40 minutes

Fabian

1　This was a great argument of love in her toward you .

2　She did show favor to the youth in your sight
only to exasperate you, to awake your dormouse valor,
to put fire in your heart, and brimstone in your liver .

3　You should then have accosted her, and with some excellent jests, fire-new from the mint, you should have bang'd
the youth into dumbness .

4　　　　　　　　　　　　　　This was look'd for at your
hand, and this was balk'd .

5　　　　　　　　　　　　　The double gilt of this oppor-
tunity you let time wash off, and you are now sail'd into
the north of my lady's opinion, where you will hang
like an icicle on a Dutchman's beard, unless you do re-
deem it by some laudable attempt either of valor or
policy

Fabian

1   This was a great argument of love in her toward you .

---

2   Shee did shew favour to the youth in your sight,
     onely to exasperate you, to awake your dormouse valour,
     to put fire in your Heart, and brimstone in your Liver :
     you should then have accosted her, and with some excel-
     lent jests, fire-new from the mint, you should have bangd
     the youth into dumbenesse : this was look'd for at your
     hand, and this was baulkt : the double gilt of this oppor-
     tunitie you let time wash off, and you are now sayld into
     the North of my Ladies opinion, where you will hang
     like an ysickle on a Dutchmans beard, unlesse you do re-
     deeme it, by some laudable attempt, either of valour or
     policie .

- Fabian seems to have a very clever way of presenting fake bad news—as essentially with onrushed enthusiasm, and speaking it as simply as possible without any elaboration, as with both the short unembellished opening sentence

  "This was a great argument of love in her toward you."

  and the only surround phrase of the speech

  " : this was look'd for at your hand, and this was baulkt : "

- He also has a fine sense of when to play the emotional card and when to let the facts speak for themselves.

- Thus, as Fabian attempts to justify Olivia's behaviour with Cesario, the onrushed F #2 opens with emotion (0/4, the first two lines) to reinforce the facts that Andrew should, as a result, put 'fire in your Heart, and brimstone in your Liver (2/0 in jus one line).

- And then his ability to add extra uneasiness by calm talk comes into play once more with the two and a half 'unembellished' line suggestion of how Andrew should have 'accosted' Olivia with 'jests' and then banged Cesario into 'dumbnesse' (the only released word in the passage).

- Only then do intellect and emotion join, as he impresses on Andrew how desperate the situation now is (3/5 the last five lines of the speech).

Twelfe Night, or what you will

Antonio

Let me speake a little . This youth that you see heere,
between 3.4.359–373

Background: believing that he has saved Sebastian from a duel with Sir Andrew Aguecheek, Antonio has been arrested for brawling in the street—in fact he has saved Viola (her disguise as Cesario fooling him as everyone else). In the first speech, having lent Sebastian his purse, Antonio asks Viola/Cesario for its return, which of course she cannot do though she is willing to share what little money she has on her. From her refusal, Antonio believes Sebastian has rejected him in his hour of need, and in his second part of the speech vehemently denounces the Cesario/Viola persona believing it to be Sebastian.

Style: one on one address in front of a larger group

Where: a public street

To Whom: the arresting officers, plus Toby, Andrew, and Fabian in front of and about Viola/Cesario

# of Lines: 12

Probable Timing: 0.40 minutes

Antonio

1   Let me speak a little .

2   This youth that you see here
I snatch'd one- half out of the jaws of death,
Reliev'd him with such sanctity of love,
And to his image, which [methought] did promise
Most venerable worth, did I devotion .

---

3   But O, how vild an idol proves this god !

4   Thou hast, Sebastian, done good feature, shame .

5   In nature, there's no blemish but the mind ;
None can be call'd deform'd but the unkind .

6   Virtue is beauty, but the beauteous evil
Are empty trunks o'er-flourish'd by the devil .

Lead me on .

Antonio

1   Let me speake a little .

2   This youth that you see heere,
     I snatch'd one halfe out of the jawes of death,
     Releev'd him with such sanctitie of love ;
     And to his image, which [me thought] did promise
     Most venerable worth, did I devotion .

     _____

3   But oh, how vilde an idoll proves this God :
     Thou hast Sebastian done good feature, shame .

4   In Nature, there's no blemish but the minde :
     None can be call'd deform'd, but the unkinde .

5   Vertue is beauty, but the beauteous evill
     Are empty trunkes, ore-flourish'd by the devill .

     _____

6   Leade me on

- The surround phrases suggest the honesty from which Antonio's seemingly justified anger stems, is coming from a very moral place, as, reversing the order in which the two sentences are set, F #4 and #3 show.

    " . In Nature, there's no blemish but the minde : /None can be call'd deform'd, but the unkinde ." (F #4)

    " . But oh, how vilde an idoll proves this God : /Thou hast Sebastian done good feature, shame . " (F #3)

- The speech starts emotionally (0/4, the first three lines of the speech), with the need to speak heightened by the very short opening sentence.

- Then the ensuing (emotional) semicolon points to how upset Antonio is, yet F #2's last two unembellished lines expressing his own foolishness in worshipping outward appearances, show that no matter how painful the images may be, he still manages to maintain his dignity, at least for a moment,

- for then comes the passionate explosion as Antonio publicly denounces Sebastian for doing 'good feature, shame' (2/3 the two lines of F #3), and while there is a modicum of intellect retained during the first maxim (1/2, F #4), the final maxim becomes emotional once more (0/3, the two lines of F #5).

- And just as the short sentence emotional opening seemed awkward and demanding, so too the very short final instruction 'Leade me on.' (0/1, F #6).

The Winter's Tale
Old Shepheard

I would there were no age betweene ten and . . .
3.3.59–78

Background: close to the spot where Antigonus abandoned the daughter of Leontes and Hermione, this is the first speech for the character, and as such it is self-explanatory.

Style: solo

Where: somewhere on the shores of Bohemia

To Whom: self, and direct audience address

# of Lines: 19

Probable Timing: 1.00 minutes

Take Note: The Old Shepheard seems to have an interesting style when something important occurs to him, for he often seems to conclue an idea, or push forward the start of a new one by means of surround phrases—as with his fury with the 'boylde-braines' young men whose hunting caused his sheep to stray (ending F #1); the knowledge of where his sheep might be (ending F #2)—possibly a pleasant realisation since it begins with an emotional ; F #5's discovery of the child; the fact that the child is not dressed warmly enough (the end of F #6); and the need for the advice of his son (all of F #7).

Old Shepheard

1   I would there were no age between ten and
three and twenty, or that youth would sleep out the rest ;
for there is nothing (in the between) but getting wen-
ches with child, wronging the ancientry, stealing,
fighting—hark you now !

2   Would any but these boil'd-
brains of nineteen and two and twenty hunt this wea-
ther ?

3   They have scar'd away two of my best sheep,
which I fear the wolf will sooner find [than] the master .

4   If any where I have them, 'tis by the seaside, brow-
ing of ivy .

5   Good luck, and't be thy will !

6   What have
we here ?

7   Mercy on's, a barne ?

8   A very pretty barne!

9   A
boy, or a child, I wonder ?

10   A pretty one, a very pretty
one : sure some scape .

11   Though I am not bookish, yet I
can read waiting-gentlewoman in the scape .

12   This has
been some stair-work, some trunk-work, some
behind-door work .

13   They were warmer that got this,
[than] the poor thing is here .

14   I'll take it up for pity, yet
I'll tarry till my son come ; he hallow'd but even now .

15   Whoa-ho-hoa .

Old Shepheard

1　I would there were no age betweene ten and
three and twenty, or that youth would sleep out the rest :
for there is nothing (in the betweene) but getting wen-
ches with childe, wronging the Auncientry, stealing,
fighting, hearke you now : would any but these boylde-
braines of nineteene, and two and twenty hunt this wea-
ther ?

2　　　　They have scarr'd away two of my best Sheepe,
which I feare the Wolfe will sooner finde [then] the Mai-
ster ; if any where I have them, 'tis by the sea-side, brou-
zing of Ivy .

3　　　　　　Good-lucke (and't be thy will) what have
we heere ?

4　　　　　　Mercy on's, a Barne ?

5　　　　　　　　　A very pretty barne ; A
boy, or a Childe I wonder ?

6　　　　　　　　　(A pretty one, a verie prettie
one) sure some Scape ; Though I am not bookish, yet I
can reade Waiting-Gentlewoman in the scape : this has
beene some staire-worke, some Trunke-worke, some
behinde-doore worke : they were warmer that got this,
[then] the poore Thing is heere .

7　　　　　　　　　Ile take it up for pity, yet
Ile tarry till my sonne come : he hallow'd but even now .

8　Whoa-ho-hoa .

- Given the releases that come later in the speech, the relative calm in the first two lines (0/1) is surprising, and might suggest that the character is exhausted from looking for his missing sheep.

- But then comes the (traditional-old-man-complaining-about-the-young) emotional explosion at the young idiots who have caused two of his sheep to go missing (1/6, the last five lines of F #1).

- And though the facts of what has occurred and where he may find them then get added in, he still remains highly emotional (4/7, F #2).

- The initial discovery of what turns out to be the child is heightened by being both emotional (0/2, F #3) and set as the first of three successive short sentences, which then turns to passion (3/3, F #4-5) as he realises that what he has found is a baby—which seems to push him into a state of great calm (perhaps trying not to wake the child) for the first two unembellished closer examination phrases of F #6.

- And then, as he comes to believe that the child is a result of a 'Scape' by some 'Waiting-Gentlewoman', so he becomes intellectual (4/1, lines two and three of F #6), but this quickly turns into emotion as he elaborates on the 'behinde-doore worke' in the child's conception, and its lack of warm clothing (2/10 in the three lines ending F #6).

- After all the bluster, his decision to protect the child is very quietly taken (0/1, F #7), though F #8's apparent yell to his son may wake the baby up!

The Tempest
Ariel

To every Article .
between 1.2.195–215

Background: Prospero created the opening tempest in order to both frighten and separate the various parties on-board so as to deal with them more easily. Ariel, Prospero's main confidant and chief controller of all the other spirits at Prospero's command, had some very specific tasks to perform without which Prospero's plans cannot come to fruition. The following is a response to Prospero's direct question 'Hast thou, Spirit,/Perform'd to point, the Tempest that I bad thee'.

Style: as part of a two-handed scene, with a third person sleeping on-stage

Where: unspecified, but somewhere close to Posprero's cell and close to Caliban's cave

To Whom: Prospero, in front of the sleeping Miranda

# of Lines: 19

Probable Timing: 1.00 minutes

Take Note: That Ariel is more a spirit of instant response and emotion rather than considered intellectual logic can be seen not simply in the releases throughout the speech, but also that, within the major punctuation, there are five emotional semicolons to just one colon, and just three surround phrases.

Ariel

1   To every article .

2   I boarded the King's ship ; now on the beak,
    Now in the [waist], the deck, in every cabin,
    I flam'd amazement .

3   Sometime I'd divide,
    And burn in many places ; on the topmast,
    The yards and boresprit, would I flame distinctly,
    Then meet and join .

4   Jove's lightning, the precursors
    O'th'dreadful thunder-claps, more momentary
    And sight-outrunning were not ; the fire and cracks
    Of sulphurous roaring, the most mighty Neptune
    Seem to besiege, and make his bold waves tremble,
    Yea, his dread trident shake .

    _____

5   Not a soul
    But felt a fever of the mad, and play'd
    Some tricks of desperation .

6   All but mariners
    Plung'd in the foaming brine, and quit the vessel ;
    Then all afire with me, the King's son, Ferdinand,
    With hair up-staring (then like reeds, not hair),
    Was the first man that leapt ; cried, "Hell is empty,
    And all the devils are here"

Ariel

1　To every Article .

2　I boorded the Kings ship : now on the Beake,
　Now in the [Waste], the Decke, in every Cabyn,
　I flam'd amazement, sometime I'ld divide
　And burne in many places ; on the Top-mast,
　The Yards and Bore-spritt, would I flame distinctly,
　Then meete, and joyne .

3　　　　　　　　　　　　　　　Joves Lightning, the precursers
　O'th dreadfull Thunder-claps more momentarie
　And sight out-running were not ; the fire, and cracks
　Of sulphurous roaring, the most mighty Neptune
　Seeme to besiege, and make his bold waves tremble,
　Yea, his dread Trident shake . {}

───────────

4　Not a soule
　But felt a Feaver of the madde, and plaid
　Some tricks of desperation ; all but Mariners
　Plung'd in the foaming bryne, and quit the vessell ;
　Then all a fire with me the Kings sonne Ferdinand
　With haire up-staring (then like reeds, not haire)
　Was the first man that leapt ; cride hell is empty,
　And all the Divels are heere .

- After the very careful short F#1 reassuring Prospero he has done exactly as commanded (1/0), Ariell's reporting of the overall details is very passionate (8/10 in F #2's five and half lines…

- …while the vainglorious comparison of his own appearances to that of 'Jove's Lightning' is somewhat more restrained, and slightly more intellectual than emotional (4/2, five and half lines of F #3).

- The surround phrases seem those of a triumphant (child-like?) story-teller—the first of which opens F #2 (logical thanks to the colon), announcing success ' . I boorded the Kings ship : '; the second is emotional (thanks to the semicolon), explaining how he kept safe the minor characters with no part to play in the ensuing unfolding of events, ' ; all but Mariners/Plung'd in the foaming bryne, and quit the vessell ; '; the last, that ends the speech, deals with the successful separation of Ferdinand, who ' ; cride hell is empty,/And all the Divels are heere . ', from those who are to be punished.

- Thus it's not surprising that the F #4 build-up to all but 'Mariners' quitting the vessel because they all 'felt a Feaver of the madde' is emotional (2/5), enhanced by two closely set emotional semicolons, and the description of Ferdinand's separation, one of the prime objectives he had to perform, also remains emotional (3/5, the last three and a half lines of the speech).

Gonzalo

Had I plantation of this Isle my Lord,
between 2.1.144–168

Background: described by Prospero both as a 'Noble Neopolitan' and 'Holy Gonzalo', Gonzalo is doing anything he can to bring Alonso, the King of Naples, distraught at the apparent drowning death of his son Ferdinand, back into a sense of current reality and responsibility so as to unite the increasingly bickering fragmented group (the two factions being the darker forces of Anthonio and Sebastian on the one hand, and the leaderless remainder, including 'good' Gonzalo, on the other).

Style: one on one address in front of a larger group

Where: unspecified, somewhere on the island

To Whom: Alonso, in front of Sebastian, Anthonio, Adrian and Francisco, and an unspecified number of 'others'

# of Lines: 19

Probable Timing: 1.00 minutes

Take Note: This sequence is often played as one long boring blab, yet F's orthography clearly shows a key difference in conception and realisation between (the discoveries of?) F #2 and (the resultant reverie of F #3).

Gonzalo

1 Had I plantation of this isle my lord—

And were the king on't, what would I do ?

2 I'th' commonwealth I would, by contraries,
Execute all things ; for no kind of traffic
Would I admit ; no name of magistrate ;
Letters should not be known; riches, poverty,
And use of service, none ; contract, succession,
[Bourn], bound of land, tilth, vineyard none ;
No use of metal, corn, or wine, or oil;
No occupation, all men idle, all ;
And women too, but innocent and pure ;
No soveraignty—

All things in common nature should produce
Without sweat or endeavor : treason, felony,
Sword, pike, knife, gun, or need of any engine,
Would I not have ; but nature should bring forth,
Of it own kind, all foison, all abundance,
To feed my innocent people .

3 I would with such perfection govern, Sir,
T'excel the golden age .

Gonzalo

1　Had I plantation of this Isle my Lord {,}

And were the King on't, what would I do ?

2　I'th'Commonwealth I would (by contraries)
Execute all things : For no kinde of Trafficke
Would I admit : No name of Magistrate :
Letters should not be knowne : Riches, poverty,
And use of service, none : Contract, Succession,
[Borne], bound of Land, Tilth, Vineyard none :
No use of Mettall, Corne, or Wine, or Oyle :
No occupation, all men idle, all :
And Women too, but innocent and pure :
No Soveraignty .

3　All things in common Nature should produce
Without sweat or endevour : Treason, fellony,
Sword, Pike, Knife, Gun, or neede of any Engine
Would I not have : but Nature should bring forth
Of it owne kinde, all foyzon, all abundance
To feed my innocent people .

4　I would with such perfection governe Sir :
T'Excell the Golden Age .

- In trying to get Alonso's attention, Gonzalo opens quite intellectually (4/0, F #1 and the first line and half of F #2), but once the idea of ruling by 'contraries' is voiced, so his pattern completely changes.

- The lengthy F #2 itemising how this would work is composed entirely of ten surround phrases, and whether this is an attempt to get through to the distracted Alonso, or is indicative of his own mind running rampant with the somewhat revolutionary ideas (though modern editors suggest that this passage is meant as a criticism of the rather startling propositions of the French philosopher Montaigne) is up to each actor to decide.

- The first explorations in the denial-of-status-distinction ideas from 'For no kinde of Trafficke/Would I admit' through to 'And use of service, none', is passionate (4/3 in just three lines), and then moving into concerns of business and the impact of the new order on human beings becomes intellectual (11/3, the last five lines of F #2).

- And with F #3's utopian overview, the surround phrases, if such still can be said to exist, become much longer, and though the suggestion that 'Nature' should be allowed to develop without 'sweat or endevour' still remains intellectual (6/3, the first three and half lines of F #3), the shift into the idealistic hope that 'Nature should bring forth/ Of it owne kinde' becomes (delightedly?) emotional (1/3).

- F #4's intellectual, surpassing the 'Golden Age', finale (4/2) is heightened by being expressed once again via two surround phrases.

The Tempest

Anthonio

{I} did supplant {my} Brother Prospero,
between 2.1.269 - 296

Background: whatever his own agenda (probably to stop paying tribute to Alonso for his help in supplanting Prospero), Anthonio seems hell-bent on persuading Sebastian, Alonso's younger brother, to oust Alonso as King of Naples, just as he, Anthonio, usurped Prospero's throne. One note: line 17's 'Sir Prudence' is a belittling term for Gonzalo.

Style: as part of a two-handed scene in front of a larger sleeping group

Where: unspecified, somewhere on the island

To Whom: Sebastian, in front of the sleeping Alonso, Gonzalo, Adrian, Francisco, and unspecified 'others'

# of Lines: 22

Probable Timing: 1.10 minutes

Take Note: Here Anthonio presents a very interesting method of persuasive attack to get what he needs - a sudden flurry of surround phrases to introduce or fortify the point he wants accepted, and then he relaxes somewhat so the other person can seemingly make their own decision.

Anthonio

1 {†} {I} did supplant {my} brother Prospero {,}
    And look how well my garments sit upon me,
    Much feater [than] before .

2   My brother's servants
    Were then my fellows, now they are my men .

3 {†}   {As for my} conscience {,}
  {†} Ay, sir ; where lies that ?

4   If 'twere a kibe,
    'Twould put me to my slipper ; but I feel not
    This deity in my bosom .

5   Twenty consciences,
    That stand 'twixt me and Milan, candied be they,
    And melt ere they molest!

6   Here lies your brother,
    No better [than] the earth he lies upon,
    If he were that which now he's like—that's dead,
    Whom I with this obedient steel, three inches of it,
    Can lay to bed for ever ; whiles you, doing thus,
    To the perpetual wink for aye might put
    This ancient morsel, this Sir Prudence, who
    Should not upbraid our course .

7   For all the rest,
    They'll take suggestion as a cat laps milk;
    They'll tell the clock, to any business that
    We say befits the hour .

---

8   Draw together ;
    And when I rear my hand, do you the like,
    To fall it on Gonzalo .

Anthonio

1 {†} {I} did supplant {my} Brother Prospero {,}
    And looke how well my Garments sit upon me,
    Much feater [then] before : My Brothers servants
    Were then my fellowes, now they are my men .

2 {†}   {As for my} conscience {,}
    {†} I Sir : where lies that ?

3   If 'twere a kybe
     'Twould put me to my slipper : But I feele not
     This Deity in my bosome : 'Twentie consciences
     That stand 'twixt me, and Millaine, candied be they,
     And melt ere they mollest : Heere lies your Brother,
     No better [then] the earth he lies upon,
     If he were that which now hee's like (that's dead)
     Whom I with this obedient steele (three inches of it)
     Can lay to bed for ever : whiles you doing thus,
     To the perpetuall winke for aye might put
     This ancient morsell : this Sir Prudence, who
     Should not upbraid our course : for all the rest
     They'l take suggestion, as a Cat laps milke,
     They'l tell the clocke, to any businesse that
     We say befits the houre . {→}

---

4   Draw together :
     And when I reare my hand, do you the like
     To fall it on Gonzalo .

- In his attempt to seduce Sebastian, Anthonio gets straight to the point with a highly intellectual description of seizing and enjoying power (5/2, F #1).

- F #2's dismissal of 'conscience' starts a little more carefully, via a careful short sentence (1/0) composed of surround phrases; but having begun to put aside Sebastian's possible objection and potential fear, Anthonio swiftly moves into overwhelm mode as he disavows any possibility of such an abstract notion standing 'twixt me, and Millaine,' passionate intellect and emotion hard at work for F #3's first four and half lines (6/4).

- Introducing the idea of killing both King Alonso (Sebastian's brother) and his advisor Gonzalo ('This ancient morsell'), Anthonio becomes totally emotional (0/5 the next five and half lines), though his further scornful description of Gonzalo as 'Sir Prudence' becomes momentarily intellectual (2/0).

- While his dismissal of the remainder as taking 'suggestion, as a Cat laps milke' turns emotional once more (1/4, the last three lines of F #3).

- And, apparently having succeeded in moving Sebastian to action, the last sentence becomes careful (1/1, F #4), the first phrase containing a moment of emotional encouragement to strike (via the word 'reare'), the second one of specific fact (directing Sebastian's murderous act towards 'Gonzalo').

The Tempest

Prospero

Now my charmes are all ore-throwne,
Epilogue 1–20

Background: with outstanding matters resolved, his Dukedom restored, his daughter and Ferdinand to be married, Ariel and his fellow spirits released, Caliban seeking for 'grace', and reconciliation with Alonso, Prospero asks the audience to release him so that he may journey back to Milan. Romantics tend to regard this speech as Shakespeare's personal farewell to the theatre. Bolding in the First Folio text suggests magic—see the commentary and Appendix 3.

Style: solo

Where: both the island and the theatre

To Whom: direct audience address

# of Lines: 20

Probable Timing: 1.00 minutes

Take Note: The six sentences most modern texts present show a very rational Prospero, far from the Folio, where an ungrammatical period puts an early end to F #1, and the onrushed F #2 is usually split into three. However, in human terms the 'incorrect' period is very important, allowing Prospero a much needed personal break following his admission he no longer has magical powers. Though he says he has no more magic left, much of the speech, as shown by the bolded text, shows him still using the spoken patterns of magic and incantation.

EPILOGUE: spoken by Prospero

1   Now my charms are all o'erthrown,
    And what strength I have's mine own,
    Which is most faint .

2   Now 'tis true,
    I must be here confin'd by you,
    Or sent to Naples.

3   Let me not,
    Since I have my dukedom got,
    And pardon'd the deceiver, dwell
    In this bare island, by your spell,
    But release me from my bands
    With the help of your good hands .

4   Gentle breath of yours my sails
    Must fill, or else my project fails,
    Which was to please .

5   Now I want
    Spirits to enforce, art to enchant,
    And my ending is despair,
    Unless I be reliev'd by prayer,
    Which pierces so, that it assaults
    Mercy itself, and frees all faults .

6   As you from crimes would pardon'd be,
    Let your indulgence set me free .

EPILOGUE: spoken by Prospero

1　**Now my Charmes are all ore-throwne,**
　And what strength I have's mine owne .

2　Which is most faint : now 'tis true
　I must be heere confinde by you,
　Or sent to Naples, Let me not
　Since I have my Dukedome got,
　And pardon'd the deceiver, dwell
　In this bare Island, by your Spell,
　But release me from my bands
　With the helpe of your good hands :
　Gentle breath of yours, my Sailes
　Must fill, or else my project failes,
　Which was to please : Now I want
　Spirits to enforce : Art to inchant,
　And my ending is despaire,
　Unlesse I be reliev'd by praier
　Which pierces so, that it assaults
　Mercy it selfe, and frees all faults .

3　As you from crimes would pardon'd be,
　Let your Indulgence set me free .

- And the onrushed F #2—which joins as one his need for the audience's help; his admission for a second time that he lacks 'Art to inchant', and the realisation that only 'praier' can relieve him—suggests that now perhaps exhausted (see the previous two speeches and in this speech the F #2 opening 'Which is most faint;' and add in the earlier statement 'Every third thought shall be my grave'), his ability to present himself and his needs with complete clarity is somewhat impaired.

- One of the very few unembellished lines sums up the speech completely,

  "But release me from my bands"

  and such an appeal to the audience from a man so used to power throughout the play must be both difficult and humbling, no wonder it's spoken so quietly.

- The first four lines of the speech expressing his lack of 'Charmes' and thus he may be 'confinde' (either on the island or in the theatre is up to each actor to decide) are emotional (1/5).

- The first words after the ungrammatical F #1 ending period are set as an unembellished monosyllabic surround phrase which suggests the acknowledgement of being 'faint' is both difficult to admit and may well be very accurate.

- Yet the idea of being 'sent to Naples' as the alternative to being 'confinde' is voiced intellectually (5/1 the next four lines), but after the unembellished line discussed above the speech becomes somewhat quieter, his fear of his 'project' failing culminating in the sad surround phrase repetition of ' : Now I want/Spirits to enforce : Art to inchant…' only slightly passionate (3/2 in five lines), the sentence end of his 'despaire' being relieved by 'praier' becoming emotional once more.

- And, possibly with tiredness claiming him once more, the speech ends quietly intellectually with a plea for the audience's 'Indulgence' (1/0, F #3).

BIBLIOGRAPHY

AND

APPENDICES

The most easily accessible general information is to be found under the citations of *Campbell,* and of *Halliday.* The finest summation of matters academic is to be found within the all-encompassing *A Textual Companion,* listed below in the first part of the bibliography under *Wells, Stanley and Taylor, Gary* (eds.)

Individual modem editions consulted are listed below under the separate headings 'The Complete Works in Compendium Format' and 'The Complete Works in Separate Individual Volumes,' from which the modem text audition speeches have been collated and compiled.

All modem act, scene, and/or line numbers refer the reader to *The Riverside Shakespeare,* in my opinion still the best of the complete works, despite the excellent compendiums that have been published since.

The F/Q material is taken from a variety of already published sources, including not only all the texts listed in the 'Photostatted Reproductions in Compendium Format' below, but also earlier individually printed volumes, such as the twentieth century editions published under the collective title *The Facsimiles of Plays from The First Folio of Shakespeare* by Faber & Gwyer, and the nineteenth century editions published on behalf of The New Shakespere Society.

The heading 'Single Volumes of Special Interest' is offered to newcomers to Shakespeare in the hope that the books may add useful knowledge about the background and craft of this most fascinating of theatrical figures.

PHOTOSTATTED REPRODUCTIONS OF THE ORIGINAL TEXTS IN COMPENDIUM FORMAT

Allen, M.J.B. and K. Muir, (eds.). *Shakespeare's Plays in Quarto.* Berkeley: University of California Press, 1981.

Blaney, Peter (ed.). *The Norton Facsimile (The First Folio of Shakespeare).* New York: W.W.Norton & Co., Inc., 1996 (see also Hinman, below).

Brewer D.S. (ed.). *Mr. William Shakespeare's Comedies, Histories & Tragedies, The Second/Third/Fourth Folio Reproduced in Facsimile.* (3 vols.), 1983.

Hinman, Charlton (ed.). *The Norton Facsimile (The First Folio of Shakespeare)*. New York: W.W.Norton & Company, Inc., 1968.

Kokeritz, Helge (ed.). *Mr. William Shakespeare 's Comedies, Histories & Tragedies*. New Haven: Yale University Press, 1954.

Moston, Doug (ed.). *Mr. William Shakespeare's Comedies, Histories, and Tragedies*. New York: Routledge, 1998.

MODERN TYPE VERSION OF THE FIRST FOLIO IN COMPENDIUM FORMAT

Freeman, Neil. (ed.). *The Applause First Folio of Shakespeare in Modern Type*. New York & London: Applause Books, 2001.

MODERN TEXT VERSIONS OF THE COMPLETE WORKS IN COMPENDIUM FORMAT

Craig, H. and D. Bevington (eds.). *The Complete Works of Shakespeare*. Glenview: Scott, Foresman and Company, 1973.

Evans, G.B. (ed.). *The Riverside Shakespeare*. Boston: Houghton Mifflin Company, 1974.

Wells, Stanley and Gary Taylor (eds.). *The Oxford Shakespeare, William Shakespeare , the Complete Works, Original Spelling Edition,* Oxford: The Clarendon Press, 1986.

Wells, Stanley and Gary Taylor (eds.). *The Oxford Shakespeare, William Shakespeare, The Complete Works, Modern Spelling Edition.* Oxford: The Clarendon Press, 1986.

MODERN TEXT VERSIONS OF THE COMPLETE WORKS IN SEPARATE INDIVIDUAL VOLUMES

The Arden Shakespeare. London: Methuen & Co. Ltd., Various dates, editions, and editors .

Folio Texts. Freeman, Neil H. M. (ed.) Applause First Folio Editions, 1997, and following.

The New Cambridge Shakespeare. Cambridge: Cambridge University Press. Various dates, editions, and editors.

New Variorum Editions of Shakespeare. Furness, Horace Howard (original editor.). New York: 1880, Various reprints. All these volumes have been in a state of re-editing and reprinting since they first appeared in 1880. Various dates, editions, and editors.

The Oxford Shakespeare. Wells, Stanley (general editor). Oxford: Oxford University Press, Various dates and editors.

The New Penguin Shakespeare . Harmondsworth, Middlesex: Penguin Books, Various dates and editors.

The Shakespeare Globe Acting Edition. Tucker, Patrick and Holden, Michael. (eds.). London: M.H.Publications, Various dates.

SINGLE VOLUMES OF SPECIAL INTEREST

Baldwin, T.W. *William Shakespeare's Petty School.* 1943.

Baldwin, T.W. *William Shakespeare's Small wtin and Lesse Greeke.* (2 vols.) 1944.

Barton, John. *Playing Shakespeare.* 1984.

Beckerman, Bernard. *Shakespeare at the Globe, I 599-1609.* 1962. Berryman, John. *Berryman 's Shakespeare.* 1999.

Bloom, Harold. *Shakespeare: The Invention of the Human.* 1998. Booth, Stephen (ed.). *Shakespeare's Sonnets.* 1977.

Briggs, Katharine. *An Encyclopedia of Fairies.* 1976.

Campbell, Oscar James, and Edward G. Quinn (eds.). *The Reader's Encyclopedia of Shakespeare. 1966.*

Crystal, David, and Ben Crystal. *Shakespeare's Words: A Glossary & Language Companion.* 2002.

Flatter, Richard. *Shakespeare's Producing Hand.* 1948 (reprint).

Ford, Boris. (ed.). *The Age of Shakespeare.* 1955.

Freeman, Neil H.M. *Shakespeare's First Texts.* 1994.

Greg, W.W. *The Editorial Problem in Shakespeare: A Survey of the Foundations of the Text.* 1954 (3rd. edition).

Gurr, Andrew . *Playgoing in Shakespeare's London.* 1987. Gurr, Andrew. *The Shakespearean Stage, 1574-1642.* 1987. Halliday, F.E. *A Shakespeare Companion.* 1952.

Harbage, Alfred. *Shakespeare's Audience.* 1941.

Harrison, G.B. (ed.). *The Elizabethan Journals.* 1965 (revised, 2 vols.).

Harrison, G.B. (ed.). *A Jacobean Journal.* 1941.

Harrison, G.B. (ed.). *A Second Jacobean Journal.* 1958.

Hinman, Charlton. *The Printing and Proof Reading of the First Folio of Shakespeare.* 1963 (2 vols.).

Joseph, Bertram. *Acting Shakespeare.* 1960.

Joseph, Miriam (Sister). *Shakespeare's Use of The Arts of wnguage.* 1947.

King, T.J. *Casting Shakespeare's Plays.* 1992.

Lee, Sidney and C.T. Onions. *Shakespeare's England : An Account Of The Life And Manners Of His Age.* (2 vols.) 1916.

Linklater, Kristin. *Freeing Shakespeare's Voice*. 1992.

Mahood, M .M. *Shakespeare's Wordplay*. 1957.

O'Connor, Gary. *William Shakespeare: A Popular Life*. 2000.

Ordish, T.F. *Early London Theatres*. 1894. (1971 reprint).

Rodenberg, Patsy. *Speaking Shakespeare*. 2002.

Schoenbaum. S. *William Shakespeare: A Documentary Life*. 1975.

Shapiro, Michael. *Children of the Revels*. 1977.

Simpson, Percy. *Shakespeare's Punctuation*. 1969 (reprint).

Smith, Irwin. *Shakespeare's Blackfriars Playhouse*. 1964.

Southern, Richard. *The Staging of Plays Before Shakespeare*. 1973.

Spevack, M. *A Complete and Systematic Concordance to the Works Of Shakespeare*. 1968-1980 (9vols.).

Tillyard, E.M.W. *The Elizabethan World Picture*. 1942.

Trevelyan, G.M. (ed.). *Illustrated English Social History*. 1942.

Vendler, Helen. *The Art of Shakespeare's Sonnets*. 1999.

Walker, Alice F. *Textual Problems of the First Folio*. 1953.

Walton, J.K. *The Quarto Copy of the First Folio*. 1971.

Warren, Michael. *William Shakespeare, The Parallel King Lear 1608-1623*.

Wells, Stanley and Taylor, Gary (eds.). *Modernising Shakespeare's Spelling, with Three Studies in The Text of Henry V*. 1975.

Wells, Stanley. *Re-Editing Shakespeare for the Modern Reader*. 1984.

Wells, Stanley and Gary Taylor (eds.). *William Shakespeare: A Textual Companion*. 1987.

Wright, George T. *Shakespeare's Metrical Art*. 1988.

HISTORICAL DOCUMENTS

Daniel, Samuel. *The Fowre Bookes of the Civile Warres Between The Howses Of Lancaster and Yorke*. 1595.

Holinshed, Raphael. *Chronicles of England, Scotland and Ireland*. 1587 (2nd. edition).

Halle, Edward. *The Union of the Two Noble and Illustre Famelies of Lancastre And Yorke*. 1548 (2nd. edition).

Henslowe, Philip: Foakes, R.A. and Rickert (eds.). *Henslowe's Diary*. 1961.

Plutarch: North, Sir Thomas (translation of a work in French prepared by Jacques Amyots). *The Lives of The Noble Grecians and Romanes*. 1579.

APPENDIX 1:
GUIDE TO THE EARLY TEXTS

A QUARTO (Q)

A single text, so called because of the book size resulting from a particular method of printing. Eighteen of Shakespeare's plays were published in this format by different publishers at various dates between 1594-1622, prior to the appearance of the 1623 Folio.

THE FIRST FOLIO (F1)'

Thirty-six of Shakespeare's plays (excluding *Pericles* and *Two Noble Kinsmen,* in which he had a hand) appeared in one volume, published in 1623. All books of this size were termed Folios, again because of the sheet size and printing method, hence this volume is referred to as the First Folio. For publishing details see Bibliography, 'Photostated Reproductions of the Original Texts.'

THE SECOND FOLIO (F2)

Scholars suggest that the Second Folio, dated 1632 but perhaps not published until 1640, has little authority, especially since it created hundreds of new problematic readings of its own. Nevertheless more than 800 modern text readings can be attributed to it. The **Third Folio** (1664) and the **Fourth Folio** (1685) have even less authority, and are rarely consulted except in cases of extreme difficulty.

APPENDIX 2:
WORD, WORDS, WORDS

PART ONE: VERBAL CONVENTIONS (AND HOW THEY WILL BE SET IN THE FOLIO TEXT)

"THEN" AND "THAN"

These two words, though their neutral vowels sound different to modern ears, were almost identical to Elizabethan speakers and readers, despite their different meanings. F and Q make little distinction between them, setting them interchangeably . The original setting will be used, and the modern reader should soon get used to substituting one for the other as necessary.

"I," "AY," AND "AYE"

F/Q often print the personal pronoun "I" and the word of agreement "aye" simply as "I." Again, the modern reader should quickly get used to this and make the substitution when necess ary. The reader should also be aware that very occasionally either word could be used and the phrase make perfect sense, even though different meanings would be implied.

"MY SELFE/HIM SELFE/HER SELFE" VERSUS "MYSELF/HIMSELF/HER-SELF"

Generally F/Q separate the two parts of the word, "my selfe" while most modern texts set the single word "myself." The difference is vital, based on Elizabethan philosophy. Elizabethans regarded themselves as composed of two parts, the corporeal "I," and the more spiritual part, the "self." Thus, when an Elizabethan character refers to "my selfe," he or she is often referring to what is to all intents and purposes a separate being, even if that being is a particular part of him- or herself. Thus soliloquies can be thought of as a debate between the "I" and "my selfe," and, in such speeches, even though there may be only one character on-stage, it's as if there were two distinct entities present.

UNUSUAL SPELLING OF REAL NAMES, BOTH OF PEOPLE AND PLACES
Real names, both of people and places, and foreign languages are often reworked for modern understanding. For example, the French town often set in Fl as "Callice" is usually reset as "Calais." F will be set as is.

NON-GRAMMATICAL USES OF VERBS IN BOTH TENSE AND APPLICATION
Modern texts 'correct' the occasional Elizabethan practice of setting a singular noun with plural verb (and vice versa), as well as the infrequent use of the past tense of a verb to describe a current situation. The F reading will be set as is, without annotation.

ALTERNATIVE SETTINGS OF A WORD WHERE DIFFERENT SPELLINGS MAINTAIN THE SAME MEANING
F/Q occasionally set what appears to modern eyes as an archaic spelling of a word for which there is a more common modern alternative, for example "murther" for murder , "burthen" for burden, "moe" for more, "vilde" for vile. Though some modern texts set the Fl (or alternative Q) setting, others modernise. Fl will be set as is with no annotation.

ALTERNATIVE SETTINGS OF A WORD WHERE DIFFERENT SPELLINGS SUGGEST DIFFERENT MEANINGS
Far more complicated is the situation where, while an Elizabethan could substitute one word formation for another and still imply the same thing, to modern eyes the substituted word has an entirely different meaning to the one it has replaced. The following is by no means an exclusive list of the more common dual-spelling, dual-meaning words

anticke-antique	mad-made	sprite-spirit
born-borne	metal-mettle	sun-sonne
hart-heart	mote-moth	travel-travaill
human-humane	pour-(po wre)-power	through-thorough
lest-least	reverent-reverend	troth-truth
lose-loose	right-rite	whether-whither

Some of these doubles offer a metrical problem too, for example "sprite," a one syllable word, versus "spirit." A potential problem occurs in *A Midsummer Nights Dream,* where the modern text s set Q1's "thorough," and thus the scansion pattern of elegant magic can be established, whereas F1's more plebeian "through" sets up a much more awkward and clumsy moment.

The F reading will be set in the Folio Text, as will the modern texts' substitution of a different word formation in the Modern Text. If the modern text substitution has the potential to alter the meaning (and sometimes scansion) of the line, it will be noted accordingly.

PART TWO: WORD FORMATIONS COUNTED AS EQUIVALENTS FOR THE FOLLOWING SPEECHES

Often the spelling differences between the original and modern texts are quite obvious, as with "she"/"shee". And sometimes Folio text passages are so flooded with longer (and sometimes shorter) spellings that, as described in the General Introduction, it would seem that vocally something unusual is taking place as the character speaks.

However, there are some words where the spelling differences are so marginal that they need not be explored any further. The following is by no mean s an exclusive list of word s that in the main will not be taken into account when discussing emotional moments in the various commentaries accompanying the audition speeches.

(modern text spelling shown first)

and- &	murder - murther	tabor - taber
apparent - apparant	mutinous - mutenous	ta'en - tane
briars - briers	naught - nought	then - than
choice - choise	obey - obay	theater - theatre
defense - defence	o'er - o're	uncurrant - uncurrent
debtor - debter	offense - offence	than - then
enchant - inchant	quaint - queint	venomous - venemous
endurance - indurance	reside - recide	virtue - vertue
ere - e'er	Saint - S.	weight - waight
expense - expence	sense - sence	
has - ha's	sepulchre - sepulcher	
heinous - hainous	show - shew	
I'11 - Ile	solicitor - soliciter	
increase - encrease	sugar - suger	

APPENDIX 3:
THE PATTERN OF MAGIC, RITUAL &
INCANTATION

THE PATTERNS OF "NORMAL" CONVERSATION

The normal pattern of a regular Shakespearean verse line is akin to five pairs of human heart beats, with ten syllables being arranged in five pairs of beats, each pair alternating a pattern of a weak stress followed by a strong stress. Thus, a normal ten syllable heartbeat line (with the emphasis on the capitalised words) would read as

weak- STRONG, weak - STRONG, weak- STRONG, weak- STRONG, weak- STRONG
(shall   I   com- PARE thee TO   a   SUMM- ers DAY)

Breaks would either be in length (under or over ten syllables) or in rhythm (any combinations of stresses other than the five pairs of weak-strong as shown above), or both together.

THE PATTERNS OF MAGIC, RITUAL, AND INCANTATION

Whenever magic is used in the Shakespeare plays the form of the spoken verse changes markedly in two ways. The length is usually reduced from ten to just seven syllables, and the pattern of stresses is completely reversed, as if the heartbeat was being forced either by the circumstances of the scene or by the need of the speaker to completely change direction. Thus in comparison to the normal line shown above, or even the occasional minor break, the more tortured and even dangerous magic or ritual line would read as

STRONG - weak, STRONG- weak, STRONG - weak, STRONG
(WHEN shall WE   three   MEET   a   GAINE)

The strain would be even more severely felt in an extended passage, as when the three weyward Sisters begin the potion that will fetch Macbeth to them. Again, the spoken emphasis is on the capitalised words and the effort of, and/or fixed determination in, speaking can clearly be felt.

> THRICE the BRINDed CAT hath MEW"D
> THRICE and ONCE the HEDGE-Pigge WHIN"D
> HARPier CRIES, 'tis TIME, 'tis TIME.

UNUSUAL ASPECTS OF MAGIC

It's not always easy for the characters to maintain it. And the magic doesn't always come when the character expects it. What is even more interesting is that while the pattern is found a lot in the Comedies, it is usually in much gentler situations, often in songs *(Two Gentlemen of Verona, Merry Wives of Windsor, Much Ado About Nothing, Twelfth Night, The Winters Tale)* and/or simplistic poetry *(Loves Labours Lost* and *As You Like It),* as well as the casket sequence in *The Merchant of Venice.*

It's too easy to dismiss these settings as inferior poetry known as doggerel. But this may be doing the moment and the character a great disservice. The language may be simplistic, but the passion and the magical/ritual intent behind it is wonderfully sincere. It's not just a matter of magic for the sake of magic, as with Pucke and Oberon enchanting mortals and Titania. It's a matter of the human heart's desires too. Orlando, in *As You Like It,* when writing peons of praise to Rosalind suggesting that she is composed of the best parts of the mythical heroines because

> THEREfore HEAVen NATure CHARG"D
> THAT one BODie SHOULD be FILL"D
> WITH all GRACes WIDE enLARG"D

And what could be better than Autolycus *(The Winters Tale)* using magic in his opening song as an extra enticement to trap the unwary into buying all his peddler's goods, ballads, and trinkets.

To help the reader, most magic/ritual lines will be bolded in the Folio text version of the speeches.

ACKNOWLEDGMENTS

Neil dedicated *The Applause First Folio in Modern Type*
"To All Who Have Gone Before"
and there are so many who have gone before in the sharing of Shakespeare through publication. Back to John Heminge and Henry Condell who published *Mr. William Shakespeares Comedies, Histories, & Tragedies* which we now know as The First Folio and so preserved 18 plays of Shakespeare which might otherwise have been lost. As they wrote in their note "To the great Variety of Readers.":

> Reade him, therefore; and againe, and againe : And if then you doe not like him, surely you are in some manifest danger, not to understand him. And so we leave you to other of his Friends, whom if you need, can be your guides: if you neede them not, you can lead yourselves, and others, and such readers we wish him.

I want to thank John Cerullo for believing in these books and helping to spread Neil's vision. I want to thank Rachel Reiss for her invaluable advice and assistance. I want to thank my wife, Maren and my family for giving me support, but above all I want to thank Julie Stockton, Neil's widow, who was able to retrive Neil's files from his old non-internet connected Mac, without which these books would not be possible. Thank you Julie.

Shakespeare for Everyone!

Paul Sugarman, April 2021

Neil Freeman (1941-2015) trained as an actor at the Bristol Old Vic Theatre School. In the world of professional Shakespeare he acted in fourteen of the plays, directed twenty-four, and coached them all many times over.

His groundbreaking work in using the first printings of the Shakespeare texts in performance, on the rehearsal floor and in the classroom led to lectures at the Shakespeare Association of America and workshops at both the ATHE and VASTA, and grants/fellowships from the National Endowment for the Arts (USA), The Social Science and Humanities Research Council (Canada), and York University in Toronto. He prepared and annotated the thirty-six individual Applause First Folio editions of Shakespeare's plays and the complete *The Applause First Folio of Shakespeare in Modern Type*. For Applause he also compiled *Once More Unto the Speech, Dear Friends*, three volumes (Comedy, History and Tragedy) of Shakespeare speeches with commentary and insights to inform audition preparation.

He was Professor Emeritus in the Department of Theatre, Film and Creative Writing at the University of British Columbia, and dramaturg with The Savage God project, both in Vancouver, Canada. He also taught regularly at the National Theatre School of Canada, Concordia University, Brigham Young University.. He had a Founder's Ring (and the position of Master Teacher) with Shakespeare & Company in Lenox, Mass: he was associated with the Will Geer Theatre in Los Angeles; Bard on the Beach in Vancouver; Repercussion Theatre in Montreal; and worked with the Stratford Festival, Canada, and Shakespeare Santa Cruz.

Paul Sugarman is an actor, editor, writer, and teacher of Shakespeare. He is founder of the Instant Shakespeare Company, which has presented annual readings of all of Shakespeare's plays in New York City for over twenty years. For Applause Theatre & Cinema Books, he edited John Russell Brown's publication of *Shakescenes: Shakespeare for Two* and The Applause Shakespeare Library, as well as Neil Freeman's Applause First Folio Editions and *The Applause First Folio of Shakespeare in Modern Type*. He has published pocket editions of all of Shakespeare's plays using the original settings of the First Folio in modern type for Puck Press. Sugarman studied with Kristin Linklater and Tina Packer at Shakespeare & Company where he met Neil Freeman.